BLUEPRINTS FROM HEAVEN-WOMEN IN THE BIBLE DEVOTION & COLABORATION

Published By: T&R Birthing Books Publishing LLC

Written By: Wenona Andress, Lequita L. Young, Artisia Williams, Sara Sanchez, Kisha Jordan, Shawn Saxton, Sharday Waddell, Valeria Chamber, Brandy Burleson, Tamika Thomas, Priscilla Vargas, Barbara Slater, Dianah Kamande, Margo Williams, Chantell Stubblefield-Bagley, Liza Velasquez, Sheila Powell, Chavelia Carthen and Evangelist Rosalind Willis. Copyright©2022

To the Authors and Readers,

Heavenly Father, we come to you now in the Name of our Lord and Savior Christ Jesus.

We ask that you give divine healing now in every area of the lives of the authors and readers of this book. As this book travels near and far, we speak healing over the lives, minds, spirits, will, emotions and physical being in accordance with your order and plan over each individuals' lives. Cover Lord, with the anointing giving a new and fresh release flowing through our inner man with rivers of living water.

Let the words of this book aid in the guidance of the Holy Spirit to those who will read it. We ask for beauty for ashes, the oil of joy for mourning and the garment of praise for the spirit of heaviness that You may be glorified always. We pray that each person receives according to John 16:23, the manifestation of every healing and miracle in the body and on earth. Anoint that only your voice is heard and give a heart to understand and be led by the Holy Spirit.

As we cover each Author of this book, may the blessings of the Lord make you rich and add no sorrow. May the Lord continue to refresh you and fill you with wisdom knowledge and understanding that only He can give. That you may be able to produce the next book with the revelation and power of the Almighty Savior. We pray continued success and all these things we ask in Christ Jesus Name. Amen and amen.

Love,

Pastor & Co-Pastor Vernon & Quineshia Maden

BLUEPRINTS FROM HEAVEN-WOMEN IN THE BIBLE EDITION BOOK 2| 2022
DEVOTION & COLABORATION

DEDICATION – This book is dedicated to our mothers Barbara Fields and Rita Willis-Clay. For training us up in the way we should go. To our 6 Jewels: Terrance, Takisha, Tommy Jr, James, Verianna, and Aaliyah. And 2 Bonus Jewels: Dantreal and Desiree. And to our 13 Heartbeats (grandchildren): Deondrae, Christian, Ja'siah Lanaya, Zayden, Dantreal Jr (DJ), Landon, Jayden, JP, Arianna, Jeremiah, Moriah, and Anari.

Thanks – First and Foremost we thank the Lord and our Savior Jesus Christ for given us this vision. We like to thank all the Co-Authors who contributed to the Blueprints from Heaven book #2: **Wenona Andress, Lequita L. Young, Artisia Williams, Sara Sanchez, Kisha Jordan, Shawn Saxton, Sharday Waddell, Valeria Chamber, Brandy Burleson, Tamika Thomas, Priscilla Vargas, Barbara Slater, Dianah Kamande, Margo Williams, Chantell Stubblefield-Bagley, Liza Velasquez, Sheila Powell, and Chavelia Carthen.** Together we will take this tool all over the world. And lastly, but definitely not least we would like to thank our church home family, **Breaking Bread Ministries**, T & R Birthing Books Publishing team, and everyone who supports our ministries. May the Lord use this tool to change people all over the world. In Jesus Name!

        Love,

Elder Tommy & Evangelist Rosalind Willis

BLUEPRINTS FROM HEAVEN-WOMEN IN THE BIBLE EDITION BOOK 2| 2022
DEVOTION & COLABORATION

Table of Contents

Pg 2: Pastor Vernon and Co-Pastor Quineshia Maden- Prayer

Pg 3: Elder Tommy and Evangelist Rosalind Willis- Dedication & Thanks

Pg 5: Coach Wenona Andress- Abigail

Pg 19: Minister Lequita L. Young- Mary and Martha

Pg 27: Coach Artisia Williams- Miriam

Pg 40: Coach Sara Sanchez- Queen Esther

Pg 57: Apostle Kisha Jordan- Shunammite Woman

Pg 86: Minister Shawn Saxton- Deborah

Pg 97: Minister Sharday Waddell- Mary the mother of Jesus

Pg 108: Sister Veleria Chambers- Elizabeth

Pg 117: Elder Brandy Burleson- Rahab

Pg 124: Missionary Tamika Thomas- Sarah

Pg 135: Evangelist Priscilla Vargas- Jochebed

Pg 148: Minister Barbara Slater- Athaliah

Pg 156: Dr. Dianah Kamande- Jezebel

Pg 165: Sister Margo Williams- The Woman at the Well

Pg 176: Sister Chantell Bagley- Hannah

Pg 188: Coach Liza Velasquez- Ruth

Pg 199: Coach Sheila Powell- Candace of Meroe

Pg 206: Prophetess Chavelia Carthen- Gomer

Pg 212: Evangelist Rosalind Willis- Two Women and Two Babies

Pg 221: References

Pg 222: Notes

Coach Wenona Andress

Coach Wenona Andress is a Clinical Social Worker from Lubbock, Texas. She provides counseling in private practice for adult clients with chronic pain and illness, mood disorders, PTSD/trauma, geriatric issues, and addictive family systems. Wenona recently published a short story in Tornado Alley anthology, has written prayer articles for Intercessors for America; was a poster presenter at Pain Week 2020, and has authored workplace curricula in foster care, adoption and addiction programs. Wenona also guest blogs, writes poetry and spiritual pieces. She co-hosts a weekly "Mind and Spirit Monday" show on The Thin Line with Ken Adams at Walk By Faith Radio, Lubbock, TX. Wenona was co-editor of her college newspaper.

Abigail

When I got a nudge from God to write about Abigail, I was excited, but felt I needed a little guidance. I researched to see what was already out there... Bible studies, blogs, podcasts and videos….so much good stuff. I wondered what I could possibly add…. I prayed about it…and got a download! A letter, so to speak. But first, let's understand how we might relate to this amazing woman.

I've heard stories from many "Abigails". Today, we could easily see her being an addict's wife or the wife of a criminal. But what if Abigail was a pastor's wife? A mayor's wife? What if she was the eldest daughter in an influential family?

What if she's a women's ministry leader but her husband is not a believer? Was she abused by some Nabals as a child? Maybe she was newly married; woke up one day, realizing she married a Nabal? Maybe everything was normal until her husband got PTSD from war or developed dementia.

Maybe there's someone out there reading about the amazing Abigail, and she thinks: "*That's great for her but she doesn't have my life. And there's only one David, so where does that leave me?*"

Let's take a closer look at Abigail: What we see; and what we don't see. Some additional information on Abigail and Nabal can be found at the end.

Read 1 Samuel 25.

The story begins after the death of the prophet Samuel. David is grieving; on the run from Saul and hiding in the wilderness. Nearby, Nabal was shearing thousands of sheep in Carmel. He was a very wealthy man. But he was known to be surly, foolish, and stingy. He was also a drunkard. His wife Abigail was both intelligent and beautiful. When David's men came to ask for some provisions from Nabal, he insulted David. Abigail knew that David had protected Nabal's men as they worked nearby. Notice that she lost no time to intervene. Abigail was decisive. She rounded up resources and quickly met David with the supplies. She was humble. Despite her fear, she stood in the gap between the wrath of David and the foolishness of Nabal. She blessed David and honored his role. She even prophesied over David: success over his enemies. She pointed out that his taking vengeance on Nabal would give him a heavy burden of guilt. She reminded him that God would fight for him; and finally, she asked for him to remember her after God vindicated him. I'm sure Abigail was terrified to face Nabal; when she returned home, he was feasting, and very drunk.

She wisely waited until the next day to tell him what transpired. We don't know what it means by "his heart failed him, and he became like a stone" (verse 37). Some scholars believe it may have been a heart attack or stroke. Nevertheless, God took Nabal's life ten days later.

After he learned that Nabal died, David asked for Abigail to become his wife. Although I'm sure she was excited, she responded with complete humility.

Where in the world did Abigail get this word and this power? We know where!

A warning here: Not all men are Nabals. In fact, none of us is sinless. We all have Nabal moments. Nabal had the opportunity to follow in the footsteps of his forefather, Caleb, who was faithful and unafraid to move into the promised land. He destroyed the Anakites, who were giants. But Nabal didn't follow a great legacy. He squandered his free will.

And now for application. This is my download from God, His "Dear Abbi"-Gail letter. Put yourself in her place. **Read this letter as if it was written just for you**:

Dear Abigail:

Abigail, I knit you in your mother's womb. I have plans for you. I knew exactly how your life was going to turn out even before you took a breath. Your placement in history was not an accident.

I know your life is hard. But my eyes search the earth and I notice your ways; that you have a heart for Me. I see your good work, your generous spirit and love for others. I already know about your husband Nabal, and I have heard your many prayers. Don't keep your eyes on him, watching him, like a fly through a magnifying glass. It's a waste of time and your energy.

Keep your eyes on me. Don't diagnose him; don't judge him. That is My responsibility. You can vent or share your concerns, but don't keep complaining about him. I will take care of him. I know you want him to love me, to follow me, to do Kingdom work alongside you. But, if he won't– leave that to me. Later, Jesus would say this to his disciples who were judging: "You follow me". I know your grief and desire for a good marriage. You are lonely and feel unloved. I know you have other options:

You could just settle for a miserable life. You can hide, or even run away. But that won't help. Dan Bohi, in *Holiness and Healing* (2016), says that healing can happen in an instant, supernaturally, over time, with some type of therapy or at the end—in Heaven. Well, I will decide if my healing or delivering you from Nabal will be in one of these ways. Either way I will provide for you along the journey…according to My riches in glory.

Your focus needs to be on me. *You are not Cinderella; I am not a fairy godmother, and this is not a Hallmark movie.* I am your David, your Father, Your Husband. I know you have heard this before "let God be your husband" and that can sound so trite, so well-intentioned by certain people. But I really will be your David. David was a model for Yeshua. Let me be your husband. I will honor you. I will wash you with the Word and my Love. I am not concerned so much about you having a "happily ever after" on earth, as preparing you as my bride for my Kingdom. Yes, Nabal has built up my wrath. Put your focus on preparing your incense of prayers, gifts, and service to me and I will bless you and reform you.

I know you can't do this alone. Ask for your help from your servants, your friends, your mentors. Remember my promises. Read the stories of your sisters Rahab, Ruth, Esther, Sarah, etc.; how I provided. I even provided well for Hagar, who was the brunt of Sarah's abuse. Did I not?

I do have plans for You, Abigail. I just need you to trust me. I will deliver. Look for the opportunity. Don't let the fear of Nabal's response stop you from pursuing that degree, starting that job, doing that ministry, and being an awesome mom. Nabal may not be your resource. His shenanigans never have, and never will, thwart My purpose for you. Don't look for Nabal in your future; let go of his abusive statements in the past. Those are lies. Satan will try to cripple you with those lies. Remember I AM Sovereign overall. Look for the resources right in front of you. Look at the people around you. I need you for my Kingdom and if you always have your eyes on your pain, you won't find the work, I need you to do. It will be a great adventure!

My Banner over you is love. Let me take the yoke from you. I delight in you. I am exalted. You bring joy to me, sweet Abigail. Come away with me.

This "letter" references these verses: Jeremiah 29:11, Psalm 139:13-16, 2 Chronicles 16:9, Hebrews 12:2, James 4:2, John 21:21-22, Philippians 4:18, Ephesians 5:26, Isaiah 62.5, Revelation 5:8, Genesis 8:21, Proverbs 15:22, Jeremiah 32:17, Matthew 11:29-30, Song of Solomon 2:4-10

Questions for the reader or prayer partners:

1. How do you react to conflict and crisis? Do you freeze? Fight? Run away? Complain? Blame? What is your normal reaction?

_____

_____

_____

_____

_____

2. Have you ever been hurt by a Nabal from your past? Do you feel like it's a wound that will not heal? Is Satan trying to convince you that you are forever crippled? Is the pain distracting you from things you would like to do?

_____

_____

_____

_____

3. If you do not relate to Abigail, do you know someone who does? Be careful, she may not be who you think she is. She might be that very successful woman you admire or the gracious older woman serving at church. Some women are not vulnerable; won't share what's really going on. They are *"FINE"* –Feelings Inside Not Expressed. How can we help one another become more vulnerable?

4. How hard is it to believe that God is really going to deal with your Nabal? What do you do if you have been praying about it for years and you see no answer? Who would you ask?

5. Speaking of helping one another, who is in your bubble? Do you have anyone you can trust to share these kinds of issues? Who is your Esther, Your Ruth, Your Sarah? How do you even go about finding them?

_____

_____

7. Women often compare themselves to other women. We can be so competitive. It's been said "Don't compare your inside to someone else's outside". Do you do this? Be honest. If you hung out with Abigail, would you find yourself lacking, embarrassed or shy? Would you be jealous? Would you be threatened at all? Would you let her into your life?

_____

_____

_____

_____

_____

8. When you hear the words that God can be your Father, Husband, or Brother, what is your reaction? Describe the word or feeling that comes to mind. Be honest. How can you grow in this area?

_____

_____

_____

8. In the letter God says Abigail is not Cinderella, He's not a fairy godmother, and life is not a Hallmark movie. What do you think is behind this statement?

9. And then there's the focus on being prepared as a Bride for His Kingdom as opposed to living for "happily ever after" on Earth. How is God preparing you to be His bride? Are you willing to do more study on that?

10. How confident are you that you, too, can be a brave Abigail? That God has a plan and adventure for you?

BLUEPRINTS FROM HEAVEN-WOMEN IN THE BIBLE EDITION BOOK 2| 2022
DEVOTION & COLABORATION

_____

_____

_____

_____

_____

_____

Prayer:

Dear God, I thank you that You are my Savior, My Lord, the Great I Am, My Master, My Abba and yes…My Husband. It is inconceivable to me that the Author of the Universe would insert me into His story. It is unbelievable that You actually have a plan that is tailored just for me! I am sorry that I am forgetful and often ignorant of Your promises, so that when trials come, or people treat me unjustly I fall to victimhood.

Sometimes I actually believe that You don't provide a way of escape. I confess that I become entranced by the world's fairy tales; when all I have to do is open my eyes to see Your Glory.

You have provided EVERYTHING I need, including the payment for my sin. Your Word says that You have supplied everything I need for faith and godliness. That means my walk here on earth, and my home in Heaven. Just think of it–I am a Bride! Along with my sisters and brothers I will be dressed in white; I will be given three new names; every tear Nabal caused will be wiped away. We will all get to feast together, and with YOU. I can't wait! Give me courage, Abba. Come away with me, my Husband. I want to rise beyond my accusers and help You get Your Kingdom ready. I'm ready for my great adventure. I am, and always will be, Your humble servant, Abigail.

Additional reading:

Abigail was from Carmel, "land of gardens". Abigail's name means "The Father Is Joyful", "Father Of Exultation". Abigail is described in the Bible as being beautiful and intelligent, and the *Aggadah* (historical texts of the Talmud by rabbis) treats Abigail as being one of the four most beautiful women in Jewish history. It's also claimed that David nearly fell in love with her while she was still the wife of Nabal, but Abigail's moral strength and dignity prevented this https://en.wikipedia.org/wiki/Nabal)

An interesting article about David's "Love at First Sight" can be found here: https://www.chabad.org/library/article_cdo/aid/3176/jewish/Love-at-First-Sight-Five-Biblical-Examples.htm

Abigail and a list of her qualities (being a true warrior, and other qualities) https://bestofchristianity.com/qualities-of-abigail-in-the-bible/

The challenge of being a "Nice" woman–*12 Women of the Bible* by Lysa TerKeurst: Session 5: *Abigail, Dealing With Confrontation* (Elise Morgan). This video can be found on PureFlix.

Also at https://2015.studygateway.com/watch/twelve-women-of-the-bible

A reading on "Trapped In A Loveless Marriage"

https://elizabethgeorge.com/blogs/devos/trapped-in-a-loveless-marriage-a-biography-of-abigail

Social history tells us that Hebrew families were very patriarchal, and women were considered property and had very few rights. But actually, Hebrew women were highly regarded. A description of women's roles can be found here https://jewsforjesus.org/learn/the-role-of-women-in-the-bible

Was Nabal a Narcissist? *3 Narcissists in the Bible-How God Took Them Out* https://poemachronicles.com/narcissists/

A great book for kids, from the Bible Belles series

https://biblebelles.com/products/abigail-the-belle-of-bravery

Minister Lequita L. Young

Minister Lequita L. Young was born and raised in Lubbock, TX; Where she served under Sr. Pastor R. L Caro, Tree of Life, C.O.G.I.C as the Youth Coordinator, Minister of Music, and Sunday School Teacher in her early years of ministry. Now, she is serving under the leadership of Bishop Reggie McDowell as Minister and Sunday School Teacher at Macedonia Baptist Church.

Lequita is Spirit-led and God-driven. She has devoted her life to God in true worship and desires to motivate, inspire, and encourage the Body of Christ to worship God in Spirit and Truth. She's a mother of three handsome boys, Isaac, Isaiah, and Elijah. She is currently pursuing her master's degree in School Counseling and works for the Lubbock School District.

Mary and Martha

Busy Breaks Relationship

Luke 10:38-42 Is about two sisters, Marry and Martha. Martha is so busy preparing dinner for Jesus. She's overwhelmed by the task of cooking to be the hostess that she forgets about her guest. At this time, she's had it with her sister Mary. At one point, her sister was helping, and she wasn't anymore. Martha found Mary sitting down while she was doing all the work. Thinking of all the things that she had to do and what others weren't doing. The cooking and cleaning that

Martha so desperately wanted Mary to help with were more important to her than sitting at the foot of Jesus.

She tells Jesus to tell Mary to help her in the kitchen. Often, we do the same thing we take on commitments that end up being overwhelming, and then we ask God for others to help us with the things we have caused ourselves. Martha was doing what she thought was right in her eyes. Doing the task was very important, but she was doing it with her strength.

Some things that we do that are right in our eyes miss the mark on what God has asked us to do. The Bible tells us to First, Seek the Kingdom of God and all of his righteousness, and all of these things will be added unto us. Matthews 6:33 Instead of being at Jesus' feet asking what we should do, we take on things and miss the mark. Martha neglected that Jesus the Son of God was there at her house, the only one who could cure her overwhelming mind with peace. Jesus told Martha, "But one thing is needed, and Mary has chosen that good part, which will not be taken away from her."

Luke 10:42 NKJV Mary was right where Jesus wanted her and that she needed to be ministered to. If Martha stopped what she was doing and came to herself, she needed to be next to Mary. Receiving everything that she needed.

Martha neglected to realize that what she was worried about was temporary fulfillment instead of eternal substance.

The prince of peace is here not only to give us a new way of thinking but also to his peace and eternal life. Jesus reminded her that Nucleating God and the peace he gives lead us to make careless stumble on our weights. In 1st Corinthians 10:31, "Therefore, whether you eat or drink, or whatever you do, do all to the glory of God" Neglecting our spiritual walk with God causes spiritual blindness. It causes us to have no sense of direction, and it causes our minds to stray away and focus on what we are going through.

Without a relationship with God, whatever we set out to do will fail. We are distracted by things that cause our walk with God to stagnate because of the weights we choose to carry. Jesus called Martha two times to bring her up to his level. Jesus came to elevate us to be at the standard to listen and do what he has called us to be, Kingdom minded.

He calls us to come to him and to cast down care upon him. The moment you say "Yes" to the Lord is the day that your hearing will be elevated. Putting away distractions, come to Jesus and lay every burden down at his feet so he may give you rest for your mind. Just like Jesus called Martha by the name he is calling you by NAME. To remind her that she wasn't looking at the big picture.

REFLECTION & ANSWER

What weights do you carry?

_____
_____
_____
_____

Are you distracted?

_____
_____
_____
_____

What area are you neglecting?

_____
_____
_____
_____

BLUEPRINTS FROM HEAVEN-WOMEN IN THE BIBLE EDITION BOOK 2| 2022
DEVOTION & COLABORATION

What area do you need to focus on?

_____
_____
_____
_____
_____

What can you learn from Martha?

_____
_____
_____
_____
_____

When you feel overwhelmed, who do you go to God first?

_____
_____
_____
_____

What could Martha do before she got overwhelmed?

BLUEPRINTS FROM HEAVEN-WOMEN IN THE BIBLE EDITION BOOK 2| 2022
DEVOTION & COLABORATION

_____

_____
_____
_____
_____
_____

What areas in your life need improvement? What are some goals to get you started?

_____
_____
_____
_____
_____

How can you improve your walk with God?

_____
_____
_____
_____
_____

How many commitments are you committed to? How are your commitments hindering you walk or helping others?

_____

_____

_____

_____

_____

Coach Artisia Williams

I have served my country. Now, it's time for me to serve you!

Strength

My Business SAVED my Life!!! 5 years and $500K value of education, experience, and experimental learning. Bachelor's Degree in Business Administration, and I have a Certificate of Appreciation from President Obama, Korean Defense Service Medal, Army Achievement Medal/Ribbon, and More. Responsibility, Activator, Input (Research), Inclusive (adding everyone), and Learner are my strengths. Born in the Sunshine State of Florida. Good Day Sunshine!

Opportunity

I am the founder of Troops IN Treatment (Different variations, but the same concept). It gave me a reason to want to wake up in the morning. My corporate-level strategy is my treatment to a lifelong journey to tell my story and help people help themselves (My Purpose). I see obstacles, or stones, that people throw at me, and I build a bridge to get over the pain/pressure (of the world). I, personally and professionally, conduct Mentorship with a Military Mindset.

Final Thought

I have a lot of conceptual, technical, and human skills. This writing journey is an eye-opener. I have accomplished a lot, and I will practice gratitude. I will use what I learned to help me get to the next level educationally, with experience, and experimentally. I hope you enjoy my art.

From, Author Artisia.

Miriam

A Spiritual Superhero Sibling

Do you know who Miriam is? Some people do, and some people don't. Either way, that's ok. Have you ever protected someone who needed help or an advocate? Let me tell you a quick story. I was at the playground, and we, the Black students, were shipped to non-diversified schools. We had to wake up an hour early in the early 90s to go to school with people who were different from us. The intent may have initially been good, but people were fighting for funding. Educators had to meet minimum quotas of race to get school funding. The "No Child Left Behind" law was in effect. I am the oldest of 5 siblings, and we have a mixed family. Race was never an issue.

Unfortunately, the disgruntled students didn't feel that way. They would ask, "Why do we have to wake up early to go to school with white people who don't want us there?" I remember this being a heated argument amongst our peers. One day, walking from school, my brother asked, "Why is my hair different from yours?" At that moment, I experienced racism for the first time. Did you get a hint from the parable (story told to tell a lesson) just like they do in the Bible? Miriam is a sibling of someone, but who? Moses is the who. Miriam is the sibling of Moses.

Miriam is not as popular as some of her peers, subordinates, and superiors, but her role played a BIG part during essential times. You can do as the Bible say, "Study to show thyself approved unto God, a workman that needeth not to be ashamed, rightly dividing the word of truth." (2 Timothy 2:15 KJV). The scripture where she can be found is Exodus 2:1-10, Exodus 15, & Numbers 12.

The best way to understand a story is to watch and/or read it from beginning to end. There was a battle going on in Exodus 2:1-10. The infants of the undesirables were to be put to death by the river. The irony is the mother of Moses put baby Moses in the river after she could not hide him any longer (approximately 3 months). She had to disguise him, so he would not be recognized. She placed Baby Moses in a basket with pitch and slime. He was placed in the Nile River. This is where Miriam came into the picture. She watched her brother to make sure he was safe, and she wanted to know his fate. Then Pharaoh's daughter came to wash herself, and she saw the basket with Moses. The Bible describes the instant connection as a connection due to the weeping baby.

Next, Miriam thought quickly on her feet and asked the Pharaoh's daughter if she wanted a Hebrew nurse to watch after the Hebrew child. Exodus Chapter 2 verses 9-10 states, 9 And Pharaoh's daughter said unto her, "Take this child away, and nurse it for me, and I will give thee thy wages." And the woman took the child and nursed it. 10 When the child grew older, she took him to Pharaoh's daughter, and he became her son. She named him Moses, saying, "I drew him out of the water."

In comic books, this is Miriam being the superhero as she began to save the day. Protection was her Spiritual Superpower. She was saving her sibling.

Flashing back to my story, I walked with my brother every day to protect him from danger. The kids were responding to the laws of the land, but I had a heart of unity. As the sophisticated Elder, we must find innovative ways to be responsible. Inclusion is actually a gift from God. Man is defined as mankind. As an Evangelist, we must meet people where they are and bring them to the promised land. We must draw out or do what Moses is predestined to do. Moses is a play on words that is similar to the Hebrew word for draw out. This is a foreshadowing of what is to come in a future text of the Scripture.

At the beginning of Exodus Chapter 15, the Israelites praise the overthrow of their predecessors. The Earth devoured the antagonist (bad guys). Moses began rejoicing and singing to the Lord. He was a strong conscientious leader. Was he younger and evidently the favorite, or was she?

I ask my mom every chance I get, "Is my brother your favorite, or am I?" She always answers, "He's my favorite son, and you are my favorite daughter." I smile, and then say, "I am your ONLY daughter, and he is your ONLY son." She smiles and then continues what she is doing. Just like my mom has love for me, Jesus has love for us.

We get a chance to start over by doing what Pastor RJ Stevenson call the ABCs He says, "Accept, Believe, and Confess." We should accept Christ as OUR Lord and savior. Believe that he died for OUR sins and confess that Jesus Christ is Lord. This is my informal invitation to Christ.

Moses is powerful and Miriam is too. God is always consuming the enemy like he did when water demolished the enemy in Exodus 15. His people were set free from the imprisonment of Egypt.

Exodus 15 KJV states, "20 And Miriam the prophetess, the sister of Aaron, took a timbrel in her hand; and all the women went out after her with timbrels and with dances.**21** And Miriam answered them, sing ye to the Lord, for he hath triumphed gloriously; the horse and his rider hath he thrown into the sea. When you are in the world, life may seem confoundedly clever."

Miriam in this case reassures her brother. The people are in good spirits due to Miriam's Superpower of celebration and praise. She stands by his side and affirms what he is doing. She leads praise. Miriam performs as a leader to the women in this passage of the Bible. She invites other women to join in the festivities of joy. She prophesies and acts as an advocate for the Lord. Even though the people became bitter for finding no fresh water. People were grumbling, and they were angry. The people were perplexed, and they were troubled. Verse **23 states,** "And when they came to Marah, they could not drink of the waters of Marah, for they were bitter: therefore, the name of it was called Marah."

Exodus 15 ends with Moses receiving direction because he cried out to God. He spares the people from going through the same pain as their predecessors (The Egyptians), and people before them. They needed joy because Miriam prepared them for a time of trouble.

We know that we can praise and worship, and then life happens. What do you do when times are hard? Do you have fear or do you have faith? This may be a simplistic question, but there are times that you may worry or fear the unknown. This is the time that one must praise and worship as The Spiritual Superpower.

God got His people going through the wilderness to appear lost. There was a plan in order. There was a 3-day journey. He wanted to test the faith of the believers, so they could have a testimony. Sometimes, due to OUR choices, we are surrounded by mess so it can eventually be OUR message. Just do like RJ Stevenson says, do the ABCs.

For the purposes of this book, the last scripture is from Numbers 12. Miriam and Aaron were gossiping about Moses' wife because she was Cushite. Cushite definition and meaning (n.d.) state, "Cushite is an "Ancient country of northeastern Africa in the Nile valley south of Egypt." Moses was humble. God came down and revealed himself. Numbers 12 Verse 5 in the Bible states "**5** And the Lord came down in the pillar of the cloud, and stood in the door of the tabernacle, and called Aaron and Miriam and they both came forth."

Miriam was in the wrong; therefore, she was punished. Just like Superman's weakness is kryptonite, Miriam's weakness was gossip. You shouldn't speak ill of your brothers and sister in Christ. God has wrath against sinful humanity. Romans 1:18-31 states, "The wrath of God is being revealed from heaven against all the godlessness and wickedness of people, who suppress the truth by their wickedness…"

The Bible states in Numbers 12: "**10** When the cloud lifted from above the tent, Miriam's skin was leprous—it became as white as snow. Aaron turned toward her and saw that she had a defiling skin disease…"

Just as God was not pleased, he punished Miriam with denied her access to the camp for 7 days, and the people waited for her return. 7 is the number of completion. We see the number 7 in the number of days in a week, 7 trumpets played, 7 priests, 7 archangels, 7 Passover days, and more.

This lets you know that God shows wrath, but God also forgives. Since 7 is the number of completion, I have successfully completed this chapter.

REFLECTION & ANSWER

1. Who was Miriam?

_____

_____

_____

_____

_____

2. Why was Moses put in the basket?

BLUEPRINTS FROM HEAVEN-WOMEN IN THE BIBLE EDITION BOOK 2| 2022
DEVOTION & COLABORATION

_____

_____

_____

_____

_____

3. What was Miriam's Spiritual Superpower?

_____

_____

_____

_____

4. What does it take to be saved (Hint ABCs)?

_____

_____

_____

_____

5. What do you do when times are hard?

BLUEPRINTS FROM HEAVEN-WOMEN IN THE BIBLE EDITION BOOK 2| 2022
DEVOTION & COLABORATION

_____

_____

_____

_____

_____

_____

6. Why was Miriam jealous of Moses?

_____

_____

_____

_____

_____

7. What was Miriam's kryptonite or weakness?

_____

_____

_____

_____

_____

8. What happened to Miriam?

9. Is God a forgiving God?

10. Do you remember my story about when I was an advocate?

Take a moment to review the chapter to answer these questions. I hope you enjoy reading the material as much as I had writing the material. You can contact me at Tint2020.com. If you refer someone to my website, you will receive a gift. Make sure you take a picture with the book to share, so we know you care.

Coach Sara Sanchez

Blessings, my name is Sara Sanchez, and I am married to an awesome man named David for almost 20 years, yes, thanks be to God, as he led me to the LORD almost 14 years ago, love you, Beloved! We have been fitted for one another by God's grace and intentionally sent out to do God's will like many of us. Amen. We have eight beautiful, anointed children and have had the honor to be their parents. MiRose, Leilani, David III, Moriah, Destiny, Sara Joy, Lil Wah Micah, and Baby Honey. I love you with all my heart and take heed in answering the call every time I think of you all. My true inspiration lent to me by our Heavenly Father. Praise be to God!

I am so thankful for my salvation, my life, all my family, my beautiful mother Stella Gallardo and best mother-in-law ever Arminda Sanchez, my late Papa David Sanchez Sr., my friends, and those who have poured into me throughout this journey called life.

I am especially grateful for this great opportunity to co-author in this divine book with all these amazing writers! I want to give honor where honor is due to Mrs. Rosalind Willis who has been a huge blessing in my life. God bless you today and always in all that you do. May God continue to give you the Blueprints from Heaven my precious sister.

God bless you and your family, and I pray all those who read this book be transformed, renewed, delivered, healed, restored and may Gods' will be done in their lives. AMEN.

Prophetic Activation to Answer the Call

Have you ever had a passion for something that you just felt the need to do with urgency? Even if others thought you were out of your element? When you mentioned it to your family, friends, or colleagues they would just laugh it off and say, "Girl you so crazy!" I mean this thing that God has birthed deep down within you, YOU just can't seem to shake it off! You think about it day and night, all the time, you have even prayed about it and you just know God has called you to do it. It is so serious that you know if you don't respond that many lives would literally be at stake!

Well…I am here to tell you today as your read this chapter that you are in a KAIROS moment. God is shifting the atmosphere just for you. He is STILL requesting more of you, to a purpose bigger than yourself, to a peculiar destiny, an indescribable vision given in this very moment to answer the call. [KAIROS: a time when conditions are right for the accomplishment of a crucial action: divine, the opportune and decisive moment.]

Father, in the name of Jesus, let our spiritual ears hear and take heed.

Esther 4:14 AMP – "For if you remain silent at this time, liberation and rescue will arise for the Jews from another place, and you and your father's house will perish [since you did not help when you had the chance]. And who knows whether you have attained royalty for such a time as this [and for this very purpose]?"

Queen Esther

You see there was this woman in the bible named Esther (put your name here) who was a beautiful Jewish girl who lived in Persia (put the name of your city here). Esther was raised by her family member named Mordecai because she was without parents to care for her. Mordecai taught Esther how to pray, fast and live out Godly principles as he helped prepare Esther for life.

She later became Queen and married King Xersus. Along the way, Esther discovered that an evil man named Haman was out to plot and kill her people. Now back in those days, Esther had to have permission to see her own husband the King and could not just see him whenever she wanted to, or she could be killed for coming to him unannounced.

Esther decided to put her faith and hope into what she had been taught all her life. Esther knew that this was the only way she could save her people, so she decided to fast and seek God in what to do even if it meant risking her own life.

During this time of prayer and fasting, God equipped her to be brave, courageous, and bold to tell the king all she had discovered. After informing the king about the evil plot of Haman he was put to death and the king gave Esther favor and granted her request to save her people.

Now I don't know about you, but I began to relate to Esther as I too was raised in a broken home with a single mother and grandparents who helped to raise me. I also saw how she was in fear to go to the king and tell him what was going on with the adversary which in this passage of the bible was named Haman. I mean how many times in life do we have someone, something or a HAMAN trying to stop us or take us out!? You see fear will always try to come in and paralyze your faith.

When I was younger fear always paralyzed me and held me captive with no voice. I mean a lot of the times I felt unqualified when I was younger. Maybe it was because it was due to all the trauma I encountered as a child. Abandoned and abused or maybe as a teen molested and raped looking for a way out to be saved or to be rescued.

But whatever it was and whatever it may be today when we start to feel unqualified because of our childhood traumas, absent parents or grieving over our loved ones, broken homes, brokenness, and more from this life. But the minute we surrender the FEAR over to God, He will give YOU healing, restoration, transformation, and the blueprint straight from heaven just like he did for Esther!

God took Esther (put your name right here) to a place where no one thought she was qualified to be at. Oh, c'mon somebodyyyyyyy, a royal place! Then he equipped her through prayer and fasting to do what he called her to do (put that calling that God has given you right here). Esther was empowered by the Holy Spirit as she fasted in a place of refuge and strength in the presence of God where she would get the very directives on how to approach the mandate, the calling on her life! ANDDDDDDD was given favor (Esther 7:3)!

Sometimes it is going to be scary, and it will feel impossible to step out in FAITH (Hebrews 11:1 / 2 Corinthians 5:7) and do what God has called you to do but be encouraged beloveds that you have been called, chosen, and all things are possible when you believe (Mark 9:23).

Now, I'm sure Esther's vision for her life was not linked up with God's plan (Jeremiah 29:11). Maybe her vision was not that big as a young girl. Maybe she just wanted to be raised by her parents and have a normal life. But what is a normal life? A normal life to God is something that bursts out His glory from one's pain (Isaiah 66:9) into another's life to help them birth their future.

It's in those very trying times of spiritual warfare and breakthrough that we can help set others free! Through perseverance and Esther's spiritual breakthrough of her God-given bold radical faith, and God's authority through prayer and fasting (Matthew 17:21 / 1 Thessalonians 5:17) Esther overcame the spiritual warfare (Ephesians 6:10-12) of her enemies, the enemies of her people, God's people.

You see sometimes you will be tested and tried in what God has called you to do and that's okay. There are times when God will ask you to do things that are difficult, yet Esther was determined, and she trusted that God sovereignly put her in that position at that time to do what needed to be done.

At this point, her faith was tested, and tried, and God was working it all for her good as she was called according to HIS PURPOSE (Romans 8:28). Trust God and the heartbeat he has given you for His people, for the calling upon your life, and His very purpose and watch God show up and show out (Proverbs 3:5-6)!

Esther (put your name right here, yes YOU) you have been called to obtain royalty for a time such as this (write the calling, the purpose, the mandate God has called you to do right here). Believe it and receive it – the calling to write that book, to start that business, to talk to those youth in detention centers, or women in prisons, speak at foster homes, pioneer reservations, bring civility to nations, and/or become that advocate in the courtroom. To do what He has called only YOU TO DO - awww… come on somebody!

God takes ordinary people. I know you have heard this before hallelujah, to do extraordinary things! The underdog, the misfit, the misunderstood, rich, or poor the WHOEVAHHHH. God is speaking through me, to you, and to all the HAMANS today. I have called Esther (put your name here) for this very time and speak over her life no more doubt, no more fear, no more what ifs, should haves or could haves, for you my beautiful Esther (put your name here) have been made a co-heir, a royal priesthood, God's Queen! Anything that God has called you to do he has anointed you to do so and set the captives free (Isaiah 61). He has given you prophetic activation to answer the call, but I ask you … WILL YOU ANSWER THE CALL? YES!

Here are some tips to ANSWER THE CALL: Declare, Decree, and prophecy them today.

• Pray – Get ready! Get excited for God to release prophetic influence of favor over your life! Esther 7:3, 1 Thessalonians 5:17-18, Matthew 17:21 – dig deeper generational curses broke!

- Declare / Decree – Open your mouth and speak it into existence! Romans 4:17

- Fast / Prophecy – Break your limitations, catch the very Blueprint from Heaven! Esther 4:15-16

- Lay your Life down – John 15:13

- Meditate – Joshua 1:8

- Faith – 2 Corinthians 5:7 / Hebrews 11:1 / Matthew 17:20

- Self-discipline – 2 Timothy 1:7

- Suit up - Ephesians 6:11

- Confident in authority – Luke 10:19

PROPHETIC ACTIVATION (IMPARTATION) TO ANSWER THE CALL

Let's pray: Father God I pray those that read this chapter hear what the Spirit is saying for it is not by might, nor by power but by Your Spirit sayeth the LORD in Jesus name we pray (Zechariah 4:6) AMEN.

➢ What does the Bible say about activating your faith? Your faith will be active and effective when your spirit woman is firm and strong as Romans 12:2 says, be transformed by the renewing of your mind.

➢ Romans 1:11 AMP - For I long to see you so that I may share with you some spiritual gift, to strengthen you and establish you.

➤ Timothy received an impartation of a gift and the anointing of God through prophecy and the laying of the hands, and the Word of God reads, 1 Timothy 4:14 AMP – "Do not neglect the spiritual gift within you, [that special endowment] which was intentionally bestowed on you [by the Holy Spirit] through prophetic utterance when the elders laid their hands on you [at your ordination]."

➤ In the apostolic-prophetic movement, a prophecy is simply a word delivered by the utterance of the Holy Spirit that accurately communicates God's "thoughts and intention."

This is what Esther received while in prayer and fasting the very thoughts and intention!

BE ENCOURAGED! Sometimes "YOU gotta encourage yo' self!" Acts 2:25

✓ I AM forgiven

✓ I AM capable

✓ I AM set apart

✓ I AM healed

✓ I AM loved

✓ I AM beautiful

- ✓ I AM His masterpiece

- ✓ I AM chosen

- ✓ I AM appointed

- ✓ I AM teachable

- ✓ I AM a willing vessel

- ✓ I AM royalty, a royal priesthood

- ✓ I AM anointed to set the captives free

- ✓ I AM born for a time such as THIS!

REFLECTION & ANSWER

1. What has God called you to do?

_____

_____

_____

_____

_____

2. Has God given you directives through fasting and prayer?

_____

_____

BLUEPRINTS FROM HEAVEN-WOMEN IN THE BIBLE EDITION BOOK 2| 2022
DEVOTION & COLABORATION

_____

_____
_____
_____

3. Have you written it down and asked Him for the blueprint?

_____
_____
_____
_____
_____

4. Has God given you a burden for His people like Esther?

_____
_____
_____
_____

5. What can you do to fulfill the vision or calling on your life?

_____
_____
_____

6. How can you relate to Esther and her courageous acts?

7. Did you feel a connection to this chapter? Why or why not?

8. Esther risked her own life for her people, for others, can you?

9. Esther received favor - Are you walking in God's favor?

10. Are you ready to answer the call?

As believers we are all available to answer the call, but the choice is ultimately up to us to do so like Esther did. I pray you have been empowered, encouraged, and even challenged to either seek for your calling or to make a decision that would bring our Heavenly Father glory and save souls which distribute God's love! Blessings to you and all attached to you! In God's Will!

Mrs. Sara Sanchez is a World Civility Ambassador, Transitional Life Coach, Faith-Based Life Coach, Founder and Chief Executive Officer of non-profit organization PROJECT 911. International Best Selling Co-Author Book STAY ALIVE Vol. 3, President of Native Education for over 6 years for the Title VI Program working with Tribal Reservations and Indigenous People, Gang Mentor for Education and Intervention Specialist, Suicide Prevention and Awareness, Child Abuse Overcomer and Advocate, Youth Nations Advocate, Restorative Justice Specialist. She is currently obtaining an associate degree in Early Childhood Education and Teacher for Children's Ministry at LWITD here in Indio, California.

Here are some scriptures that have inspired me along my journey!

"I can do all things through Christ who strengthens me" – Philippians 4:13

"She believed she could, so she did" – Proverbs 31:25

"God is within her she will not fail" – Psalm 46:5

"She is clothed with strength and dignity, and she laughs without fear of the future. –

Blessed is she who believed, for there will be a fulfillment of those things which were told to her from the LORD." – Luke 1:45

"Blessed be the LORD, my rock, who trains my hands for war, and my fingers for battle." – Psalm 144:1

"Be still and know that I am God." – Psalm 46:10

"Pray without ceasing."– 1 Thessalonians 5:17

"Trust in the LORD with all your heart and lean not on your own understanding, in all your ways submit to him, and he will make your paths straight." – Proverbs 3:5-6

"Create in me a clean heart, oh God, and renew a steadfast spirit within me. Do not cast me away from Your presence, and do not take Your Holy Spirit from me." - Psalm 51:10-11

"Three things will last forever faith, hope, and love and the greatest of these is love."– 1 Corinthians 13:13

"You intended to harm me, but God intended it for good to accomplish what is now being done, the saving of many lives." – Genesis 50:20

"Then you will call upon Me and go and pray to Me, and I will listen to you. And you will seek Me and find Me, when you search for Me with all your heart." – Jeremiah 29:12-13

"Consequently, he is able to save to the uttermost those who draw near to God through him, since he always lives to make intercession for them." – Hebrews 7:25

"We love because he first loved us." – 1 John 4:19

Apostle Kisha Jordan

APOSTLE KISHA hails from East Orange, New Jersey, and is the daughter of Grace Thompson, who has gone home to be with the Lord. Apostle Kisha is married to an anointed and awesome man of God, Dr. Jerome D. Jordan. These middle school sweethearts have been married for more than 30 years and together for more than 38 years. Together they have three beautiful daughters Kendra, Keona, and Kenya Jordan.

On Christmas day of 1989, Apostle Kisha's life took a dramatic turn, as she was involved in a near-fatal car accident. On the way to the hospital, her heart stopped twice. As a result of the injuries sustained in the accident, Apostle Kisha had her entire right leg and a portion of her pelvis removed. She spent several days in a coma, endured many life-threatening procedures, and countless hours of rehabilitation until she was finally discharged from Bay Front Medical Center three months later on March 30, 1990.

At the time of the accident, only her oldest daughter, Kendra, was born. Doctors informed her that as a result of the injuries she should not bear any more children and that any attempt to do so would kill her. But God bestowed His favor upon her, and she gave birth to her daughters, Keona, and Kenya.

Shortly thereafter in 1992, while stationed with her husband at Fort Rucker, Alabama, Apostle Kisha accepted the Lord as her savior. The miracle-working power of God would again triumph over the word of the doctors who said that it would be impossible for her to be fitted with a prosthesis. Apostle Kisha defied the odds, as God blessed her with a prosthesis worth over $10,000.00, paid for by the Fort Rucker Alabama Non-Commissioned Officers Association.

In 1994, she sensed that God was calling her into the gospel ministry. After two years of preparation, she was licensed into the gospel ministry as an evangelist. On April 2, 1996, she moved with her husband to Hawaii, to complete his tour of duty in the United States Army. Then in May 1997, God called her husband into the pastoral ministry, as the pastor of Pentecostal Central Christian Church of Hawaii. Apostle Kisha became the First Lady.

While working with her husband in the ministry, God blessed Apostle Kisha to oversee the Women of Holiness. From July through September 1997, Apostle Kisha was in charge of the daily operations of the church while her husband was away training with the Army. In the same year, she was installed as the Vice-President of the Oahu Chapter of the International Association of Minister's Wives and Minister's Widows located in Honolulu, Hawaii, under the direction of Dr. Celeste.

God would move again when Apostle Kisha gave her powerful testimony during an International Association of the Women Handmaiden's meeting. As a result of the word shared, He opened the door for Apostle Kisha to share her testimony with Pastor Drucilla Lewis, on her daily televised broadcast "Purpose for Living".

On October 1, 1998, Apostle Kisha was ordained as an Elder In 2001, she was elevated and installed as the President of the Oahu Chapter of the International Association of Minister's Wives and Minister's Widows. The St. Petersburg Times did an article titled, "The Remarkable Mrs. Jordan", highlighting the amazing story of Apostle Kisha's near-fatal car accident and her victory over death.

Today, God has raised this anointed vessel of the Lord to be a voice to the nations. In January 2005, Apostle Kisha appeared on the Home Keepers televised broadcast with host Arthelene Rippy on the Christian Television Network.

In August 2005, Apostle Kisha Jordan launched Kisha Jordan Ministries (KJM). A powerful media ministry reaching the lost and encouraging God's people through books, conferences, prayer meetings, radio, and television ministry. Kisha Jordan Ministries has staff and covenant partners around the world.

Apostle Kisha's book, "I Am the Lord That Healeth Thee" forwarded by Arthelene Rippy, was released in April 2006. This powerful message of hope has touched the lives of countless people around the world. In 2021, she released, "Get Delivered from the Saints". To get your copy of these books go to Amazon or you can order them through KJM.

In 2006, Apostle Kisha launched her radio show "Born for Such a Time as This" and in 2008, the show expanded to Saturday morning radio. KJM has been active, sponsoring several conferences and making donations to organizations such as the Cancer Foundation. In 2010, the ministry started sending monthly support to countries such as Kenya, Uganda, India, and now to the Philippines.

In January 2009, Apostle Kisha launched "Keeping It Real with Kisha Jordan" on one of the subsidiary stations of Bright House Networks and the Internet. Then in July 2009, the Lord opened a major door. Apostle Kisha entered a contract to host her own nationally televised show on Preach the Word Worldwide Network. The half-hour show is still on the air and can be seen all over the world on Cable, Roku, all smartphones, Internet, Google TV, Apple TV, Firestick, and many more. Furthermore, some shows are uploaded to Apostle Kisha's YouTube page. The response has been phenomenal as calls for prayer, testimonies, to support the ministry financially, and to become a covenant partner keep coming in.

In 2014, the Lord opened the door for Apostle Kisha to launch her radio show on WRXB 1590. The half-hour show titled "Real Talk with Kisha Jordan" aired on Saturdays at 1:30 pm est. Also, in 2014 the Lord opened another major door for Apostle Kisha, to be on another television network with her own television show on The Now Network which is seen all over the world.

In 2019 God yet opened another door for Apostle Kisha to have her own television station on the OnPoint Network, which airs on Sundays at 7:00 pm est. Then in 2020, God opened another global television show that airs around the world on Tuesday nights at 9:30 pm est. That same year, God opened up another great door for her second radio global broadcast which broadcast on a big station in Atlanta, Georgia. Building upon the favor of God, Kisha Jordan Ministries, provides books, as well as videotaping and publishing services.

In addition to her work with Kisha Jordan Ministries, she also oversees the "Women of Destiny" the Women's Ministry for the City of Refuge Christian Church of Florida. Apostle Kisha also runs conferences and revivals throughout the year, including her annual conferences "I Am the Lord That Healeth Thee", "The Cry that Everyone Ignored", "Wounds Made into Steppingstones" and "Get Delivered from The Saints". Then in July 2016, the Lord opened up another door for Apostle Kisha, to have her own international radio show titled "Kisha Jordan Ministries" which comes on every Tuesday morning and Thursday evening on www.kdaylive.com.

Apostle Kisha is an anointed preacher, teacher, author, and speaker known for her dynamic Bible teaching and preaching with delivery as an exhorter and motivator. She delivers a unique message that crosses denominations and cultures. This wife, mother, pastor, preacher, and evangelist is sought after from around the world, as far as India, Africa, and Hawaii. Apostle Kisha works in all the gifts of the Spirit and has a deep love for God's people and the unsaved.

After all that God had done in the life of Apostle Kisha, she has continued to defy the odds and with every passing moment, God is enabling her to walk further and further on her crutches and even further in her spirit.

All is Well

Praise the Lord for truly the Lord is worthy to be praised! When I think of the goodness of Jesus and all that He has done for me my soul cries out" Thank you, Jesus!" Look what the Lord has done.

First, I give honor to God, Jehovah that is the head of my life. Without Him, I cannot breathe or do anything. I give honor to my lover, my best friend, my doctor, my bishop, my good thing, and my husband, Dr. Jerome D. Jordan. I thank God for my daughters, our church family, and the churches under our ministry around the world. I wanted to say a great big thank you and a special shout out to Dr. Rosalind Willis for blessing me with the opportunity to be in this great book, and to your husband, your family, and to your publishing company.

Shunammite Woman

I remember when I got the call from Dr. Rosalind asking me to be a part of this book focusing on the women in the bible. I said to myself, "Oh my gosh" this should be good. There are so many great women in the bible that we can glean from. After praying and seeking the Lord to determine which lady He wanted me to write about, the Shunammite woman kept coming to me.

So today, I want to talk with you about the awesome, anointed, Shunammite woman mentioned in 2 Kings 4:8-37. I look at the Shunammite woman as a woman of exceptional faith. Faith is important because as the scriptures read in Hebrews 11:1-6, Amplified- "…faith is the assurance (title deed, confirmation) of things hoped for (divinely guaranteed), and the evidence of things not seen [the conviction of their reality—faith comprehends as fact what cannot be experienced by the physical senses]. [2] For by this [kind of] faith the [a]men of old gained [divine] approval.

[3] By faith [that is, with an inherent trust and enduring confidence in the power, wisdom, and goodness of God] we understand that the worlds

(universe, ages) were framed *and* created [formed, put in order, and equipped for their intended purpose] by the word of God so that what is seen was not made out of things which are visible. ⁴ By faith Abel offered to God a more acceptable sacrifice than Cain, through which it was testified of him that he was righteous (upright, in right standing with God), and God testified by accepting his gifts. And though he died, yet through [this act of] faith he still speaks. ⁵ By faith [that pleased God] Enoch was caught up *and* taken to heaven so that he would not have a glimpse of death, and He was not found because God had taken him; for even before he was taken [to heaven], he received the testimony [still on record] that he had walked with God *and* pleased Him. ⁶ But without faith, it is impossible to [walk with God and] please Him, for whoever comes [near] to God must [necessarily] believe that God exists and that He rewards those who [earnestly and diligently] seek Him."

    The Shunammite woman was strong in her faith. She was a woman who knew how to stay in her own lane. She was a woman that knew who she was, and she knew what she wanted. The Shunammite woman truly walked by faith. She was an insightful woman with an uncanny ability to discern that Elisha was truly a man of God. Glory be to God!

Maybe this is why her husband trusted her. He knew that his wife was an amazing and faithful woman of God. He was not afraid for her to walk in her true calling. He trusted his wife to the fullest. To do this, he had to be confident in himself. Moved by faith, she spoke to her husband and said, "Let us make a little chamber, I pray thee, on the wall. She wanted to make sure that the man of God had a place to lay his head down when he comes into town, so that the man of God, can rest during his time of traveling." Not many men would allow such a thing.

I am a firm believer that God will teach you how to treat and handle a man or woman of God. The truth of the matter is, there is a blessing when we do. As we read in the word of God:

The one who receives a prophet because he is a prophet will receive a prophet's reward, and the one who receives a righteous person because he is a righteous person will receive a righteous person's reward (Romans 10:41).

The Shunammite woman wanted to make sure that whenever the man of God traveled to her city that he had a place to eat and rest. She wanted to ensure they were well taken care of. For me, as a woman of God, who travels in service to the Lord, I thank God for people like the Shunammite woman whom God has placed in my life. I thank God that He always has someone to look after his anointed children. On this day, the Prophet Elisha was on a journey and turned into the chamber to get some rest.

Moved by her act of kindness, and her willingness to go out of her way to bless the man of God, Elisha sought to be a blessing in return. He wanted to find out a way that he can bless this woman. He said to Gehazi, his servant or as I like to refer to him, his armor-bearer, call the Shunammite. When he had called for her to come forth, the Shunammite woman came and stood at the door. This reminds me of when God calls me, without hesitation, I am standing before him saying, "Here I am".

And he said unto him, "Say now unto her, Behold, thou hast been careful for us with all of this care." Which means he was well pleased with the care that she was giving them. He said what is to be done for thee. I believe God is saying the same thing to His children today. In other words, when you seek to please the Lord, the Lord is actively seeking to see what shall be done unto you. Amen!"

After all, we serve a great and powerful God, who will not forget all that you do. In fact, the word of God says in Hebrews 6:10: "For God is not unjust. He will not forget how hard you have worked for him and how you have shown your love to him by caring for other believers, as you still do." Glory be to God, let's give God some praise!

So, the man of God wanted to be a blessing to this woman. After all, she had been such a blessing to them. After he called for the Shunammite woman, she came and stood at the doorpost. Although she was doing just fine with her position in life, she was content and comfortable. She was not looking for anyone to come and get into her business. Nevertheless, Elisha wanted to know what can be done for this woman of God who had done so much for him.

She answered and said, "I dwell among mine own people." It is as if she was politely saying to the man of God, "Please do not try to figure me out or get into my business." But what she did not understand that God was already in her business. In fact, God knows all our business as the word of God declares, in Matthew 10:30, "…the very hairs of our head are numbered". Talk about knowing our business. God knows us better than we know ourselves.

Gehazi, then confirmed to Elisha, that she did not have any children and her husband is old. We all know what Gehazi, was trying to say. With this information, the prophetic began to stir in Elisha, and he began to prophesy. I mean the real spirit of prophecy rose in him. I thank God for the real prophets that God has placed in my life. Glory be to God!

In verse 16, Elisha declared to the Shunammite woman, "About this season, according to the time of life, thou shalt embrace a son." Glory be to God.

In other words, at that moment he began to speak life into the place. He began to speak life into the void that was in this woman's life. It was a void that had been hidden for many years behind the mask she was wearing. In the latter part of verse 16, she said, "Nay. My lord, thou man of God do not lie unto thy handmaid."

To hide the hurt, she was in protective mode when it came to not having a child. She was okay with her life, and she learned how to master acting like she was okay with not having a child. You know how it is when you have been hurting so much for so long, that you do not want anyone else to give you another word. You know how it is when you get a word, and you are waiting for that word to manifest fast. But you're waiting and waiting, and it seems like it's just not coming to pass.

You know how it is when you don't really want anyone to know the pain that you are in. The pain of your waiting. You know when you really wanted something really bad, but it seems like you will never get it. You know when you have been living right and doing right, and others are getting the blessing that you are waiting on. Come on now, you all know what I am saying.

She didn't want anyone to lie to her. You know how it is. You have been waiting for something you really want, and it seems like you are not ever going to get it, so shut your want down for a little. You shut your dream down for a little. You shut down your excitement for a little bit. You shut down your faith just a little bit. You shut down your vision for a little. You begin to build bricks up around your life, your ears, your emotions, etc. because you have been let down so much. You're afraid to dream again. You're afraid to just step on the water. You're afraid to jump out on faith. Because the last time you did it. It still wasn't working for you, and you were hurt all over again.

We don't know how many times she and her husband had tried to have a baby. Now that she had put the frustration and pain of not having a child behind her, she did not want to open herself up to the pain of being a barren woman. Look we don't know this woman but we all can relate to her. We might not be childless. But there are some things we really want. Like the Shunammite woman, we have prayed and prayed, waited and waited, and even faithfully served others in the name of the Lord. And, like the Shunammite woman, it seems like we are never going to get it!

But I am here to tell you to, "Hold on!" That's the message from the Shunammite woman to you and me. The bottom line is God's got you. God knows exactly what you need. He knows when you need it. He knows how you need it. He also knows who to use to get you what you need. Glory be to God.

We serve a great and mighty God, who can do anything. This woman is about to get blessed with something that she wanted. Through the Prophet Elisha, God spoke a word into her future. Elisha wasn't afraid to speak what the Lord told him. Elisha said I have a word and I am about to release this word to you. So, he spoke the word to her and as we see in verse 17, the woman conceived and bore a son at that season that Elisha had said unto her, according to the time of life.

Let me tell you all something, it does not matter what it looks like. It doesn't matter what your haters say. It doesn't matter what the devil is doing or saying. What matters is what is God saying. Close your ears to anyone speaking foolishness. Close your ears to the false prophets. God has someone who is real that will speak an accurate, right now word into your life. Like He did for Abram, God always has a ram in the bush. Look around your bush is right by you.

At that moment Elisha spoke into this woman's life, he sent a word into her situation. He released a manifestation into her future. Elisha saw the need the Shunammite woman was trying to hide. The Shunammite woman did not want to get her hopes up anymore. She knew that her husband was up in age. She knew that everything was not working the way it was supposed to work to get a child. She just didn't want to get disappointed anymore.

Have you ever gotten to a place in life where you said don't speak another word to me? You reached that place you just did not want to be lied to anymore because you're tired of your heart getting broken. You're tired of crying and hurting. Have you ever been to that point when you wanted to be left alone? You don't want to hear anything others have to say about your situation. This must have been how the Shunammite woman was feeling. So, she pleaded to the man of God, do not lie unto thine handmaid.

You see, you have been through so much and your heart is hurting as you wait for your dream to come to pass, you began to build walls all around yourself. But there is a problem with this approach to dealing with the pains of life. Yes, it can be an effective way to stop people from getting in. Unfortunately, it will also stop you from getting out and trusting again. You become isolated in the heartache and pain.

Thank God that the words of the Shunammite woman did not discourage Elisha. He knew the God that he served. He knew who he was in God. Now, let me pause for a moment. As you are reading this chapter in this book, I need you to learn all the more who you are in God. It will make a difference in your life and unlock the realm of the supernatural in your life.

See Elisha was a real prophet, and he was holding a powerful move of God that needed to be released into the Shunammite woman's life. He was not a false or fake prophet; he was a real prophet with a real word from God that needed to be released. And when he spoke the word, the bible says in verse 17 the woman conceived, and bare a son at that season that Elisha had said unto her according to the time of life.

Someone who is reading this word right now is shouting, "There is a real prophet in the house. Glory be to God!" Come on and give our great God some praise for all the great things that He has done and is about to do in your life. Thank you, Jesus! Listen God does not lie, EVER and I am sitting here rejoicing over all the blessed words that have been spoken over my life.

Can you imagine the Shunammite woman's smile? Can you imagine her excitement when she found out that she was pregnant? When she found out that her dream had come to pass. When she realized that all her faithfulness, labor, and giving were not in vain. When she realized that God has some real prophets in this world. Can you imagine how she felt when she missed her period when she realized she was carrying life inside of her belly? When she realized that the Lord had touched and healed her husband who was too old for such a blessing had it not been for the power of God. I mean come on.

This was a miracle. Glory be to God. This was something to shout about. Thank God for this great and powerful miracle. Thank God that she finally got her dream, her heartbeat, she finally got her child, she finally got her man-child. She finally got her promise! After waiting for so long, she finally got her bouncing baby boy. To say she was excited would be an understatement. Her joy must have been unspeakable, indescribable, and at this point in her life, unfathomable. Now she knew without a shadow of a doubt, that God is a God that keeps His promises.

For twelve years, I can imagine her caring for her baby and raising him. She watched him cry, she watched him grow, she watched him roll, she watched him scoot. She watched him crawl. she watched him try to stand. She watched him try to take a step and fall. She watched him as he attempted to take one step at a time. She watched him as he developed his personality. She watched him smile. She heard him laugh, saw him cry, and wiped his tears. She saw him get upset, hurt, and happy. She felt his warm skin.

I can see her so happy being a mother. I can see her doing what real mothers do for their children, taking care of her son and praying for him. I can see her giving God praise for her dream coming true. For twelve years, I believe that she had the time of her life as a loving, nurturing mother. But, as you might have imagined, her battles were not over.

One day the Shunammite woman's son was with his father, and the bible says that the son began to talk about his head was hurting. He said, "My head, my head, my head!" The father sent him home to his mother. He had them take him to his mother and there is a reason for this.

When the child got to his mother and the bible says that he sat on his mother's knees till noon and then died. We all know that Satan will attack your dreams. He'll attack them both before and after they manifest. If given the opportunity, he will kill your dreams and visions. This is why you have to know Jesus for yourself.

What do you do when your dreams die on your lap? What do you do when your vision dies on your lap? What do you do when the gift that God has given you dies? What do you do when your promise dies in your hand? What do you do when you have waited so long for something that the Lord has promised you and it dies? What do you do when you have cried for years for something and you finally got it, only to see that it has died right before your very eyes? What do you do?

That's exactly what the Shunammite woman had to deal with. Faced with this heart-wrenching, unfortunate incident, the death of her son, she demonstrated extraordinary faith. This woman did not do the normal thing. This woman picked up her baby. She picked up her promise. She picked up her gift. She picked up her dream. She picked up the lifeless body of her baby boy. She was broken and I know that she had to have shed some tears.

With the odds stacked against her, and a bleak outlook on the situation, the Shunammite woman got the strength that could only come from God. I can hear her say, "If I can get my son to the anointed man of God?" She refused to let her promise die. Now, there's a word for the body of Christ. Regardless of the situation, refuse to let your dreams die.

Maybe something has died on your lap, maybe it was a vision, maybe it was a gift. Maybe it was a promise that God has given you and now the enemy is relentlessly attacking your promise. Maybe it was buying a home, and something went wrong. Maybe it was a job, and you lost it. Maybe your spouse walked out on you for no reason. Maybe you lost your church. Maybe your dream has finally come to pass and now it appears to be dying in the midst.

See the devil always wants you to start questioning God. The devil wants you to mock the Lord. The devil wants to make you doubt what the Lord has said over life. But the devil is a liar. The word of God tells us in John 8:44:

He was a murderer from the beginning, not holding to the truth, for there is no truth in him. When he lies, he speaks his native language, for he is a liar and the father of lies. But to the devil's chagrin, he picked the wrong mother when he attacked the Shunammite woman's son. She was a praying mother. She had the strength of God flowing through her life. Instead of giving up, walking away from her dream, and counting life as lost, she picked up her son. Walking in faith, she carried her lifeless son, her heart, and her promise up the stairs.

I can imagine that she was crying as she carried him. I can imagine her kissing him on his cold lifeless body. I can imagine her talking to the Lord as she carried the dead weight of her son up the steps. An arduous task, but she got it done. She was hurting, but despite her hurt, I believe she was still praying as she carried her promise upstairs step by step.

Notice she did not call the funeral home to come to retrieve his lifeless body to prepare it for burial. She did not call any family members or friends. She didn't even tell her husband that their son had died. Instead, she took her child upstairs and laid her promise on the bed of the anointed man of God bed. She laid him in the one place that could revive and restore her son. She laid him in the residue of the anointing that was on the bed where the man of God slept. Good God almighty!

I'm trying to keep myself together while I am typing. It's hard to shout and type at the same time, but with each word, I type I can feel a dance stirring up inside of me. Glory!

See, I can't speak for you, but I can surely speak for myself. I love hanging around those who are covered in the anointing of God. I mean the genuine and authentic anointing of God, not this fake and hypocritical stuff being passed off for the power of God. The anointing is more than just screaming, yelling, and talking loudly, while living a jacked-up, ungodly life. I am talking about truly anointed people who are living the life that they preach.

I remember ever since I was a little girl, I liked sitting around the older and much wiser woman and men of God. Women and men who were living for the Lord and lived the life that they preached. I would leave their presence feeling strong, feeling good, feeling great. I didn't know it then, but I know it now. It was the anointing. The bible said when Mary and Elizabeth met, that the baby leaped, glory be to God! Like Mary and Elizabeth, I could feel my spirit leaping inside of me.

See there is something about the anointing and God's anointed ones. And this woman knew this. She did not call anyone to tell them that her son was dead. In verse 21, "…she went up, and laid him on the bed of the man of God, and shut the door upon him, and went out." Now, this is some strong true faith.

I don't think that you all heard me. She took her dead son and carried her dead son with his cold body upstairs and laid the child on the bed of the man of God and shut the door. In other words, she knew she was coming back to pick up her promise. Glory be to God!

After she secured the room by closing the door, "…she called unto her husband, and said send me, I pray thee, one of the young men and a donkey, that I may run to the man of God, and come again." Notice that she did not tell her husband that their only son had died. She just asked him to get her transportation. Glory be to God!

The search is on now for Elisha, I can hear her saying Elisha, where are you, I am coming for you. In verse 23, her husband said, "…wherefore wilt thou go to him today? It is neither "new moon", nor sabbath. And she said, "All is well!" Good God almighty!

Remember, her promise, her heart, her only child had just died on her lap. She had just carried his cold body upstairs to the bed of the man of God's room and she shut the door and went downstairs and called her husband. Now she tells him that all is well. My God, what extraordinary faith. I want to just shout and scream, but I am on a tight timeline as I must have this manuscript submitted to Dr. Rosalind in a few hours.

But this woman had great faith and she told her husband, "All is well". What great faith and now she is on her way to look for Elisha. She saddled her donkey, and told her servant, "Drive and go forward; slack not thy riding for me, except I bid thee." She wanted to get to the man of God fast. She wanted to get to the man of God who spoke life into her barren womb. She wanted to let him know that her promise, her baby was dead.

When she got where the man of God was at Mount Carmel, he asked Gehazi, to go see what the Shunammite woman wanted. He said, "…run now, I pray thee to meet her and say unto her is it well with thee? Is it well with thy husband? Is it well with the child?" And she answered, "It is well."

Now, this just blew my mind, good God almighty! Once she got to the man of God, she showed her desperation as she caught the man of God by the feet. This mother had a need.

Have you ever had a need before? Have you ever had a desperate need? I mean the kind of need where you are searching for God. I mean a need in which you really need God to move, and you will stop at nothing until you find Him. I mean it's like a life-or-death situation and you don't know where to go or whom to turn to.

But in moments like this, here's a word to the wise. You must watch out for people who will dismiss your need. People who will try to discourage you and stop you from getting to God. This is what we see from the servant, Gehazi. The bible says he came near to the Shunammite woman to thrust her away. However, that did not stop the move of God in the Shunammite woman's life, and you should not let such misguided acts stop the move of God in your life.

Even when others are standing in the way of the move of God in your life, you must continue to say, "All is well" and keep moving forward. You see, God was working behind the scenes, through Elisha. By the revelation of God, Elisha knew something was wrong. Like the Shunammite woman, I thank God for having people in my life who have the gift of discernment and are truly anointed. Elisha said to Gehazi, "Leave her alone. For her soul is vexed within her and the Lord hath hid it from me, and not told me."

The Shunammite woman remained bold and steadfast in her faith. She was like let me cut right through this because my baby, my promise is laying upstairs in my house on his death bed. She was wounded, in pain, and tired of hurting. She said to the man of God, "Did I desire a son lord…. Did I not say do not deceive me?"

Once the man of God realized what was going on he commanded Gehazi, to gird up thy loins, and take my staff in thine hand. He instructed him if he met any man do not salute him not. Don't stop and don't even talk. Lay my staff upon the face of the child. He was trying to give him a job to do, but the Shunammite woman was not going to let Elisha, get through that fast.

She was like, "Oh no, not today Elisha". She said, "As the Lord liveth and as thy soul liveth, I will not leave thee." She was like, "The devil is a liar. I am not going anywhere. You promised me. You spoke to my child here. You're not getting off that easy." And Elisha, followed her.

Gehazi had already gone before them, and he had done just as Elisha instructed him. He laid the staff upon the face of the child. Unfortunately, there was neither no voice, nor hearing. There was nothing. But this was a job for Elisha. And, just as this was a job for Elisha, many circumstances in our lives are jobs for Jesus. Glory be to God.

Sometimes, I cry out Lord Jesus help me, and He always comes to see about me. Admittedly, as the songwriter said, "He may not come when we want Him, but He will be there right on time". Although my timing may be different from Jesus' timing, one thing is for sure: He always comes through for me.

Gehazi, then returned to the man of God after there was no success with the child. Now, it was time for Elisha, the one walking in the anointing, to step into the room where the body of the dead child had been laid. The Bible says in verse 34, "…he went in, therefore, and shut the door and prayed unto the Lord."

I can just imagine his prayer. I mean he had to be praying up a storm. Remember, he's in the room where he had been studying and praying. There must have been a powerful residue of the anointing permeating the room. This was the perfect place, the right atmosphere, for the move of God and Elisha knew it. The Bible says once he went in, he shut the door.

He shut the door for a reason. Look, when you're looking for God to work a miracle, you must remember to shut the door, and shut your mouth everyone can't go with you. You must shut the doors in your life to ensure the atmosphere in which you are expecting a move of God is not disrupted. The truth of the matter is, just as it was with Elisha, Gehazi, and the Shunammite woman, not everyone's faith is on the same level. When you are believing God for something you cannot afford to have any doubters, haters, or secret haters in the room sabotaging the move of God.

In the room, Elisha was praying to the Lord. I can imagine him talking to the Lord and saying, "Lord, please. We need a miracle. Lord, I am asking you to bring this dead child back to life." In this situation, Elisha had to do something that would have looked crazy to someone else. Look he had to shut the door, even on the child's mother. Then, if that wasn't enough, he got up and lay upon the child, and he put his eyes on his eyes. He wanted to look at this miracle. He put his hands on his hands. He wanted to make sure that he felt his hands when his hand began to warm up. He even stretched himself upon the child and the flesh of the child waxed warm.

Look at this miracle coming back to life. Look at this promise coming back to life. You know the devil was getting nervous by now. Trust me the devil recognizes those who are truly anointed of God.

Then he returned and walked in the house to and fro; and went up, and the child sneezed seven times, and the child opened his eyes. Glory be to God! The child came back to life. After being dead all that time. Good God almighty. He called the woman and gave her, her child back.

Now look at this, this woman is once again holding her promise, her child is alive! Won't God do it! Remember a key aspect of the move of God that manifested in the Shunammite woman's life, was her declaration that, "All is well". Even when it looked hopeless, she declared all is well. When her back was against the wall, she declared all is well. When others stood in her way, she declared all is well. When it looked as if God had failed her, she knew nothing could be further from the truth and she declared all is well.

In closing, here are a few scriptures regarding courage, trust, faith, and being victorious:

Have I not commanded you? Be strong and courageous. Do not be frightened, and do not be dismayed, for the Lord your God is with you wherever you go."

Trust in the LORD with all your heart, and lean not on your own understanding; In all your ways acknowledge Him, And He shall direct your paths (Proverbs 3:5-6)

The Lord is my strength and my shield; in him my heart trusts, and I am helped; my heart exults, and with my song, I give thanks to him (Psalms 28:7)

"Everything is possible for one who believes." (Mark 9:23)

Therefore, I say to you, whatever things you ask when you pray, believe that you receive them, and you will have them. (Mark 11:4)

For everyone born of God overcomes the world. This is the victory that has overcome the world, even our faith. (1 John 5:4)

Be on your guard; stand firm in the faith; be courageous; be strong. (1 Corinthians 16:13)

For more information, or if interested in being a guest on an upcoming broadcast, or to contact Apostle Kisha see the information provided below:

Facebook: www.facebook.com/kishajordanKJM
Email: kishajordanministries@yahoo.com
Twitter: http://twitter.com/KJMRealTalk
Instagram: @authorkishajordan
YouTube: www.youtube.com/KJMMinistries
Web: www.kishajordanenterprises.org
            www.theremarkablekishajordan.com

Minister Shawn Saxton

Minister Shawn Saxton MBA/BS- President/Founder of The Ramah Non-profit organization that provides gender-specific programming to girls and women, ages 10 to 65 years old. Our goal is to empower broken girls today, to become healthy whole women for tomorrow. The program target girls who are at risk of developing harmful traits, provoked from negative influences and experiences from environments unfavorable for their well beings. We want to get them early, so we won't have to work so hard on the back end.

Shawn Saxton is a longtime advocate for Domestic Violence/Intimate Partner Violence (Survivor), Suicide, Mental Health/Substance Abuse (Co-Occurring) and for Children that aged out of the state foster care systems for at-risk girls. My career has always put me in the position, to empower hurting children, girls and women wherever I am put to work. TREC, Inc., feed the homeless, provide basic needs whenever possible. We, collaborate with other organizations and churches when we're able to assist with a need. We, understand the emotional, physical and social pressures girls face and how it can influence unhealthy behavior that can transition into adolescence and adulthood. Shawn Saxton is a humanitarian who has global partnership with those who have the same vision. Shawn Saxton, Inspire, Ignited and Empowerment as a Global

Influencer. We have a mandate to go into all the world to spread the gospel and we do this by demonstrating the love of Christ.

Bible College Facilitator/ Keynote/Motivational Speaker/Certified Life/Transitional Coach/Domestic Violence, HIV Advocate/ Suicide Safe Talk facilitator/ Human Traffic Facilitator/ Trained in Substance Abuse and Mental Health groups / Entrepreneur/ Blogger / Author. International No. 1 Best Book Seller/Global Recipient of Red Blazer award of Excellence. Nominated Women of Vision Award 2021, Nominated for a Women Vigor Award 2021 and the finalist for the face of WHOA 2022.

Ms. Shawn Saxton MBA, BS

The Ramah Empowerment Center, Inc. (President/Founder)

http://www.trec4change.com

www.theramahempowermentcenter@gmail.com

PO Box 261992 Tampa, FL 33685

(813) 453-2646 (860) 800-2079

H.E. Shawn L Saxton, MBA

Licensed Minister, United Pentecostal Church International

"Deborah's Worship Carried the Anointing"

Judges 4:4-5 *And Deborah, a prophetess, the wife of Lapidoth, she judged Israel at that time. And she dwelt under the palm tree of Deborah between Ramah and Bethel in mount Ephraim: and the children of Israel came up to her for judgment.*

Worship: (N) *the feeling or expression of reverence and adoration for a deity:*

"We worship God, not man"

Deborah was a woman of great wisdom, revelation, and discernment. She was a prophet and a judge who never went to war or handled a weapon; it was her relationship with God that separated her from the other judges, and her worship got His attention. She held court under a tree that became known as the Palm of Deborah between Ramah and Bethel and the Israelites went up to her to have their disputes settled. She judged and won wars by being focused, prayerful, obedient to God, and not allowing anything to get in the way of that. She knew how to get God's attention.

Deborah was obedient to the call of God on her life and her responsibilities as a judge and a prophet. As a prophetess, she conveyed the will of God through divine means, and as a judge, she judged the Israelites to ensure they were living according to God's commands. She was sold out to the work of God to advance the kingdom. She did not try to be anyone else but who God created her to be – a prayer warrior and a strategic planner in war. She was able to get the attention of the Lord by praying and worshipping. Deborah was a worshipping warrior.

I could personally relate to Deborah as a worshipper. I have found in life that more battles were won in my worship of God, than with my hands in one-to-one combat or verbal exchanges in word battles. This has been true when I have dealt with family matters, work issues, and church matters.

(Reflection)

Consider:

What is your role in the Kingdom of God?

_____

_____

_____

_____

_____

How do fight your battles?

_____

_____

_____

_____

_____

Judges 17:6 - *In those days there was no king in Israel, but every man did that which was right in his own eyes.*

Trustworthy- (Adj)- *able to be relied on as honest or truthful.*

Deborah did not wait for a crisis, she had a consistent life of worship and prayer, and that is how she got the Lord's attention. Deborah was trusted by God as His representative; she was what God was looking for to advance the Kingdom. She knew what God was looking for and she did not operate outside of her gifting as a judge. She was the only female judge, the only one to be called a prophet, and the only one described as performing judicial functions. The bible is clear to mention there was no rebellion or uprising against Deborah. Deborah knew the order of God's word and understood authority as she worked alongside her husband. She knew her husband was in the leadership role, and she never lost sight of that even as a judge.

There are times when people will come to you or avoid you for different reasons. Many times, I have found people come to me because they know where I stand on an issue, that my conviction is unmovable, and/or they stay away because of the same reason they will come to me; and they know that I will not uphold nonsense. However, what I have come to learn is that no matter what, I must always remember who it is that I serve and to whom I am ultimately responsible.

(Reflection)

Consider:

Do you get on social media and ask ungodly people for advice concerning spiritual matters before going to God or seeking Godly counsel?

_____

_____

_____

_____

_____

Are you seeking "your truth" or the Truth?

_____

_____

_____

_____

Does your truth line up with the word of God?

_____

_____

_____

_____

God used the Prophetess Deborah because of her Worship, trustworthiness, and availability to do the work to advance the kingdom. It was said that there were no men, but that is not so. There were men who were in the nation and could have been raised up, then again, were they available? Did they have God's attention?

The Prophetess Deborah was able to command from under the Palm tree. She had a nation come to her to be judged daily. She did not wait around, she made herself available and accessible to a nation in crisis. She spoke the word of the Lord, "Have not the LORD God of Israel commanded......She reminded the men of what God instructed.

In crisis mode more often we do not know what to do, we even try to hide from the Lord. The prophetess was not trying to hide, she was willing to lead the people and the Lord empowered her as she instructed them. They wanted her to physically lead them in the battle against the Canaanite oppressors. As a judge, she had to know the law. In those days women did not rule or lead, however, the Lord chose her. Deborah did not question God's voice, nor was she concerned about what others would say.

Deborah was a worshipper, she was trustworthy, and she was accountable to God. Has the Lord called you to ministry? Are you submitted to your spiritual authority? The Lord will not use anyone that is operating outside of His authority and that cannot be found accountable.

For the Lord to trust you, you must be in a place where the Lord can see and hear you. He never had to wonder about Deborah's whereabouts. God established His authority in the book of Genesis with Adam.

Gen 3:9 - *And the LORD God called unto Adam, and said unto him, Where art thou?*

(Reflection)

Consider:

Can you ever remember a time when you tried to hide from the Lord?

_____
_____
_____
_____
_____

Are you making yourself available to God in every aspect of your life – personal, work, and church?

_____
_____
_____
_____

How do you relate to Deborah?

_____
_____
_____

Minister Sharday Waddell

Her name is Sharday, but most of her friends and family call her *Day* or *Day Day*. She will answer to any one of them. She is a mother to one son name KayCee and as of April 2, 2022 she became the wife to Russel Haynes. She answered her call in 2016 to minister under Bishop McDowell at Macedonia in Anton, Texas. She started attending that church in 2010 and moved to Lubbock, Texas in 2007.

She was born December 26, 1985, in Houston Texas. Her family moved to Anchorage Alaska when she was young. Her younger years have also been spent going back and forth to Dallas, Houston, Alaska from 1998 to 2007. She graduated from Dimond High School in 2004.

She loves working with kids. She once had her own daycare that she ran after graduating from high school. Her son was born in 2013 on July 21 while finding out that she was 11 weeks pregnant with him 2 months prior she was diagnosed as having Lupus. She was told that she should have been diagnosed at the age of 13 when she first got sick, and the doctors did not know what to call it, but they knew at the point that she needed a blood transfusion. But she says that God had her the whole time. And she knows he will not let her go any time soon at the age of 36! Her testimony still continues...

Mary the Mother of Jesus

When we look at Mary being a virgin, in her teens might not yet be in her 20s. One day will be married to a man named Joseph who is older than she is. They have not had intimate relations that bring on a baby to be born. An angel comes and tells Mary God has favored her and she will be the virgin that the Messiah will come through. She will raise him and teach him the thing God needs him to know and in time as he grows there will be a set time in history, he will save the world from their sins.

Mary asked humbly how, and the angel answered her and reassured her that God can make the impossible, possible. Her family that could not have children was also pregnant now. The angel told her what to name the child, and what it meant and why.

As Mary was pregnant Isaiah told of the Messiah, how and where he would be born. A king takes the throne and puts an in order for something that has never been done before. So, a very pregnant Mary has to travel to Bethlehem where they can't find any place to stay. But one man had a place where he kept his animals and let Joseph and Mary stay there.

Mary gave birth in something we would consider a barn, wrapped the Baby Jesus in swaddling clothes {rags}, and laid Baby Jesus in a manger {feeding trough}. The shepherds came to see baby Jesus and told Mary what the angels told them. That confirmed what God sent the angel to tell Mary.

The word said that when the days of her purification they brought Jesus to Jerusalem to present him to the Lord and they went into the temple and a man Simeon, and a lady Anna prophesied to them about who the child was and what would become of the child. The word said that Mary kept what in her heart what was said to her.

When Jesus was 12 years of age Mary and Joseph traveled to Jerusalem after a custom feast and Jesus stayed behind and they did not know of it until they were a days journey away from Jerusalem. They thought he was with their kinsman but when they went to go look, he was not in the company of any of them. So, they went back to Jerusalem, and he was in the temple preaching to the elders. They asked Jesus what he was doing, and he said to his mother, "Why did you seek me? Do you know that I must be about my father's business?" Mary was reminded of what she gave birth to.

As Mary continued to see her son grow and walk into the things that God has called him, getting closer to the end. Mary saw her son heal and do great miracles. She was aware that there were people out there that wanted to kill him.

Mary stood at the foot of her son's cross and saw him beaten, and battered she saw him bloody as if he was a criminal. Knowing that this is the very thing her child was supposed to be doing, she was still his mother here on earth. She went to the tomb where Jesus's was laid to anoint his body for a proper burial when an angel appeared letting her know he is not there and has risen.

When it comes to Mary, I feel I relate to her as God sent Angel Gabriel, telling her God favored her and she will have a virgin birth and bring into the world the one that will be the savior of all mankind. When I found out I was pregnant with my son my doctor said I should not go through with having him only because a year before I was giving the diagnosis of having Lupus, and health was not the best just yet to be giving birth to a child.

Although I was not in my teens but old enough and still young, I was in my 20's and a few other people thought the same thing. But God spoke to me and told me the child I was carrying would be alright. He will do some good things and I still have yet to find out what is all to come.

God assured me that he had me and my son and all will be well. Even now he is 9 years old and has his moments of talking back and not doing what I say, but then there is the reminder when he comes and asks to pray and read his devotional on the prayer line without a problem.

There are ups and downs in raising children and scares in trying to protect them and make sure we are being good enough examples to lead them to Christ. I cannot speak of losing a child because I have not. But I understand it is not a good feeling. And as a parent, if we know or find out someone is trying to hurt our child we will go above and beyond to make sure nothing bad come to them and protect them at all costs.

I love the song; *Mary Did You Know?* And I believe she would have answered with a "YES." She did know. The Angel, the Shepherds, Simeon and Anna, some Wisemen all came and said some things and the word of God said Mary held, pondered, treasured, all of these things in her heart.

Things happen to mothers when we are pregnant, and that baby starts to grow. We start to wonder what they will become, what will they do and what will they like. Is it a

boy or a girl, what will their favorite color be? Until that child is here, I believe God is giving and talking to us preparing us for this little one and how to raise them to be what God wants them to be.

They may not be the Savior of the world, but God has predestined us and the child or children we bring into the world, that everyone has a role to play in the kingdom of God and what God wants of them. Isaiah had already prophesied that a virgin would give birth to the Messiah. A child being born will be given up to the government. He that know no sin would become sin for us. Reconciling us back to God the Father. What role will we play?

I Pray: Lord God, help us be more like Mary by having the heart of being your servant. Find favor on us as you did with Mary to be the role of who or whatever you have called us to do and be. Lord let the person that is reading this, ask humbly how can or how will they be able to do and accomplish what you are asking of them without doubting you. Be able to say just like Mary "I am your servant, and Let it be so." Lord God, we thank you for choosing us to be your vessels. And for the women reading this Lord God, the child that she would carry and did carry you knew them first and although they may not be doing what is needed right now, you said in the scriptures, "Your Word would not come back void."

For the mother or the parents reading this that have a child that has died Lord God, heal the hurt. In your son Jesus Christ's name, we say Amen.

REFLECTION & ANSWER

1. When we Think about the mother of Jesus. What do you feel?

_____

_____

BLUEPRINTS FROM HEAVEN-WOMEN IN THE BIBLE EDITION BOOK 2| 2022
DEVOTION & COLABORATION

2. How do you think she really was feeling on the inside?

3. How would you have responded?

4. Do you think you could have said "So Let It Be."?

BLUEPRINTS FROM HEAVEN-WOMEN IN THE BIBLE EDITION BOOK 2| 2022
DEVOTION & COLABORATION

5. Do you Believe Mary understood all it meant to be Jesus' Mother?

6. Could you have taken on this task like Mary?

7. What would your response to 12year old Jesus be when he says, "Did you not know I had to be about My Father's business"?

8. Seeing your son going through all the pain of taking on the sins of the world and being on that cross. Would you have stood there like Mary did?

9. In all that we know about Mary. If it, was you would the story be any different?

10. At the end of it all can we answer Yes to the song. Mary Did You Know?

BLUEPRINTS FROM HEAVEN-WOMEN IN THE BIBLE EDITION BOOK 2| 2022
DEVOTION & COLABORATION

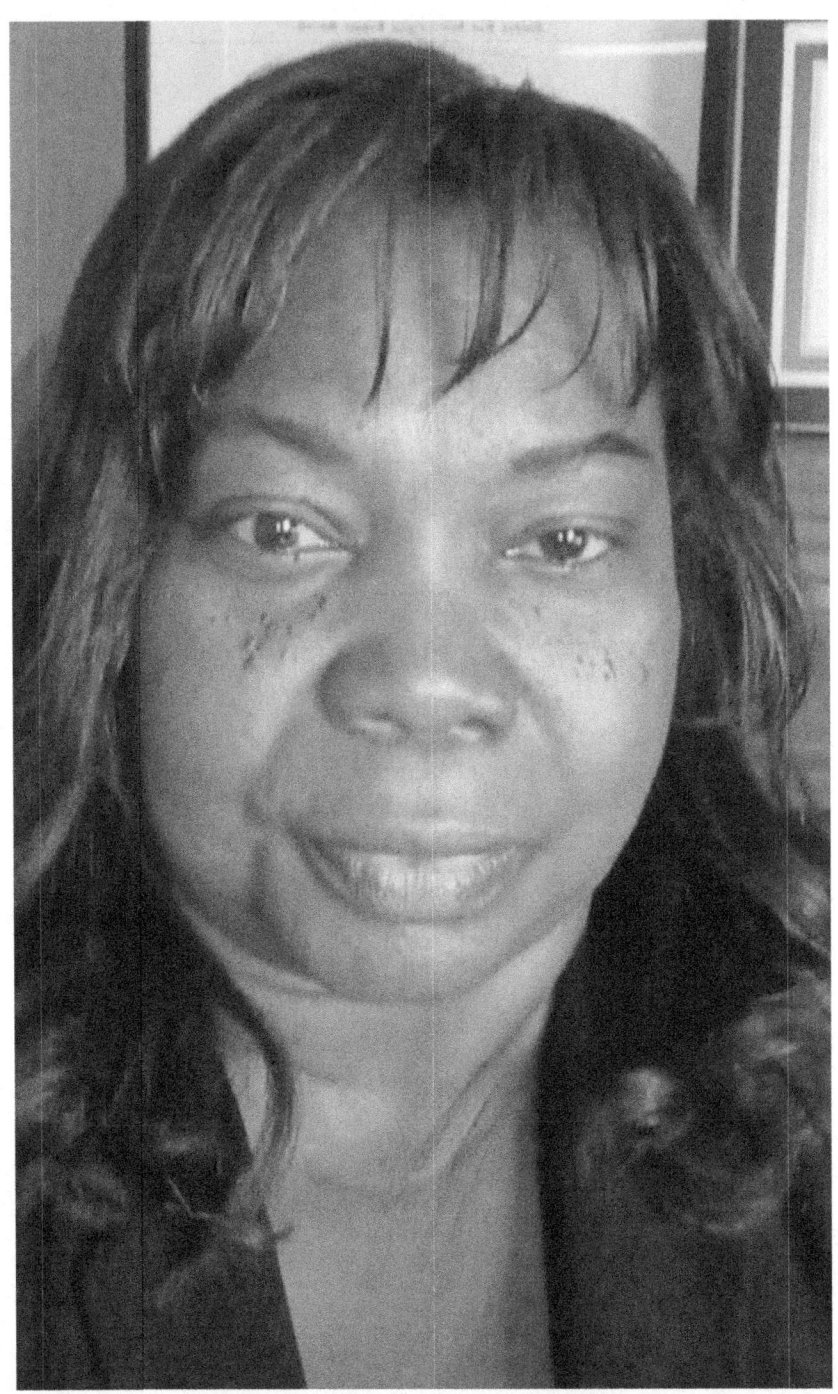

Sister Veleria Chambers

Hello and greetings. I am Veleria Chambers, MSED of Florida, the Sunshine State. I was born and raised in the USA South with both my parents. My mother will always be my Esther in spirit and in truth. She taught me how to pray and hope for the best, by bringing out the beauty in my spirit that raised me to be who I am. Her actions of love and the best affordable care transits into my life through Jesus Christ. Remember, please. Be bless to be bless and then God will make tables turn and happen in your favor again today.

Thank you ♥ -- *Dr. Rosalind Willis & Elder Tommy Willis*-CEO & Spiritual Midwives

Aunt Beth "Elizabeth"

And it came to pass, that, when Elisabeth heard the salutation of Mary, the babe leaped in her womb; and Elisabeth was filled with the Holy Ghost." (Luke 1:41 KJV)

Believe it or not, all names have a meaning. The meaning of the name depends on the region or the origin in which the name was established. Then, the name bares a definition. The definition can generate from a male or female. Usually, the definition associates with the gender of the person. The person then carries on the name given and fulfills a purpose.

The name Elisabeth is no different. Elisabeth comes from the origin of Beth, which means second. In addition, the word or name Beth reminds one of several significant cities, which is important to believers. The description of the city appears busy yet reportable at the same time. The city is known as Bethlehem.

Was Elisabeth named after the city of Bethlehem? No one really knows. Bethlehem is also a place that associates with the birth of Jesus Christ. Jesus Christ, "God's only begotten son" (John 3:16 KJV) apparently visits Beth or Bethlehem a second time. The second time is during Jesus Christ's earthly visit. The first time is in His spiritual kingdom with God, the Father. How did Jesus Christ visit Beth in His spiritual kingdom with God the father? This question may seem puzzling to nonbelievers. It should because you must believe to receive" (John 3:16 KJV). One of the best things that one can receive is to believe in Jesus Christ.

Belief in Jesus Christ does not take away from the story of Elisabeth. In fact, Jesus Christ adds to Elisabeth's, the woman of God, story. Jesus Christ gives all things life and life more abundantly (John 10:10 KJV). Yes, this section is about Elisabeth, but nothing is complete without mentioning the name of Jesus Christ, "The Son of the living God" (Mathew 16:16 KJV).

Elisabeth is the wife of Zachariah. Zachariah comes from the lineage of Aaron, a priest. Aaron was also the brother of Moses. Moses was called to deliver God's people (Exodus 3:1-3 KJV). God 's people continue to receive deliverance to date (Corinthians 1:10). Moses selects a group of men, which includes Aaron to be priests. Aaron contributions includes speaking for Moses on God's behalf. Aaron delivered messages to Pharaoh, who released the Hebrews out of Egypt (Exodus 7:12 KJV).

Now that some background has been presented, it is time to become familiar with Elisabeth. Elisabeth desires to have a child as mentioned in the settings of Luke in Chapter 1:6 King James Version (KJV). The conceptual framework in Luke 1:2 arrived from storytellers, who were not only observed but told stories to others to set the setting of this chapter. Moreover, observations of the literature in Luke Chapter 6 involves a physician. How would you describe your physician? Most physicians are detail oriented with years of study before their practice begins.

However, Luke 1:1 KJV reveals a declaration order. A declaration is an announcement. In this case, the announcement is a spiritual one. The announcement includes something that is believed. A belief, according to dictionary.com (2022) deals with the acceptance of something.

Next, verse 1:2 confirms that eyewitnesses, such as ministers were involved in this announcement. How many times have you believed that you knew something and thought, "If only I had an eyewitness to confirm?" How would you handle the issue? Would you wait for a trusting relative to visit? Well, that is exactly what Elisabeth did. Elisabeth relationship to Mary, mother of Jesus Christ varies. What is certain, is that in 1:3, Luke indicates that he has some understanding of the events that are taking place. Luke was placed in such high authority from God that he reports his findings to the Most Excellent Theophilus.

In other words, could you imagine being asked to report your findings to Vice President Kamala Harris? What about being a researcher and reporting directly to Michele Obama as an independent quality control health administrator, or an independent contractor as a researcher for Oprah Winfrey, where everybody gets something of value? You get the concept. It is an honor when someone have high regards for a person, especially person with high credentials.

Although Zacharias was a priest, a later visit from Mary was more astonishing. Elisabeth could not have children (1:7), but her husband, Zacharias, was a praying man. How many of you know that quote, "Whoso findeth a wife findeth a good thing, and obtaineth favor of the Lord a man finds a wife, he finds a good thing." (Proverbs 18:22). The conceptual framework of Luke 1:2 was aware. The angel, next to the alter, brought confirmation of an upcoming event regarding Elisabeth (1:13).

Now when the angel of the Lord spoke in Luke 1:13, trouble surfaced my mind. For one, some things in this world does not agree with the Lord. I wonder did Zacharias feel the same within his spirit. Either way, Elisabeth and her husband was going to have a son! It was time for the celebration preparations to begin. Announcements, party shakers of congratulations were in progress for all to see because Luke 1:14 suggests gladness and joy. In addition, an expression raveled the forefront. Joy filled the air that day for this child, who was to be called John (1:13)

However, some feelings of joy were short because in Luke 1:18 (KJV), Zacharias did not believe Gabriel. He was too focused on himself. How many of you focus on yourself and not the word of God? I am guilty, but God, who mercies are unconditional, covers me.

Now, let's focus more on the main character. Elisabeth and Zacharias resided in Judea. How many of you want to live in a city of praise? Did you know that Judea and Judah are the same, according to Britannica.com (2022)? Either way, Gabriel delivered the news to Mary that she had favor with God and was with child (Luke 1:31). Also, Gabriel told Mary that her cousin Elisabeth was with child (1:36). Can you say a double baby shower with the Holy Ghost power? What awesome news!

The angel Gabriel clarified that Elisabeth was Mary's cousin in Luke 1:36 (KJV). So why is this chapter entitled "Aunt Beth Elisabeth"? The title of this chapter is recognized as "Aunt Beth Elisabeth" to identify with older women who consider themselves to be an aunt, due to their age. The respect of an elder takes one on an enormous adventure. Furthermore, Elisabeth age did not stop God from using her, her husband Zacharias, and her unborn son, John the Baptist. "For with God nothing shall be impossible" Luke 1:37 (KJV).

Mary now knew that Elisabeth was six months pregnant (Luke 1:36 KJV). "And it came to pass, that, when Elisabeth heard the salutation of Mary, the babe leaped in her womb; and Elisabeth was filled with the Holy Ghost:" (Luke 1:41 KJV). So now, young Mary went to visit her relative, who she shared a bond. The bond was that they both were pregnant. Have you ever shared a bond with someone older? Well, this bond was filled with the Holy Ghost. Can you imagine having been filled with the Holy Ghost? I remember as a child how people would receive the Holy Ghost. People would just change in an instant. Whether they would fall to the floor or mop the floor with their clothes, something was evident. What I admire most is that the bond was with two women. The thought of two pregnant women praying together throughout their pregnancy is phenomenal.

And Mary abode with her about three months and returned to her own house. (Luke 1:56 KJV). The phenomenal miracle of Mary and Elisabeth shows that God place things in order. God allowed the older relative to experience a desire first. Then, he blessed Mary to have a road model of her older relative, Elisabeth. The time spent with family and friends is essential. Each day the miracle of life occurs as God breathes life into our bodies. Another extraordinary event that occurred was that God instilled His son, Jesus Christ, and the Holy Spirit among a family that prayed together. The magnitude of two women carrying on the prayer and praise service. Women today can take away so much from these two extraordinary women.

The resource tools of these experiences can be just as the scripture indicates from the book of Luke Chapter One. So many times, the words are listed directly on the pages of what the expectations are for something to occur. Zacharias was in the temple and could not see the significance of trusting God's Angel. He was not able to speak the entire pregnancy until his tongue loosed. (Luke 1:64). A picture of a celebration comes to mind with the father not able to speak, until he speaks of God's plan. God plan may not always be our plan, but if we obey God, all can participate in His celebration.

Elisabeth insisted on following directions regardless of the people's comments. She knew that she could not name the child after his father. Elisabeth was strong and did not allow the comments to change the child's name from John. When we learn that we are mere vessels for the Lord, we all can rejoice and be exceedingly glad. God will always take care of His people no matter how old or young. God is in control. One of my favorite prophecies of Zacharias is the following: "Blessed be the Lord God of Israel; for he hath visited and redeemed his people (Luke 1:68 KJV). Also, a prophecy to remain the course is "And the child grew, and waxed strong in spirit, and was in the deserts till the day of his shewing unto Israel." (Luke 1:80). Be bless.

Elder Brandy Burleson

Elder Brandy Burleson is a mother of 2 boys and a grandmother (GIGI) of 1 grandson. She is currently serving as Pastor of Intercession at Restoration Square Full Gospel Baptist Cathedral. She is also a business owner of Face Beat Cosmetics and a published author "Standing on the Promises of God." She will be graduating from Texas Southern University, with a bachelor's degree in Health Administration in 2023. After graduating, she plans on opening her own Nursing Home Clinic. She has been inducted into, Phi Sigma Pi Honors Fraternity, TSU Honors Program, Honor Society and The National Society of Leadership and Success.

Rahab

You Counted me Out, But GOD Counted Me In!

"And Joshua the son of Nun sent two men secretly from Shittim as spies, saying, 'Go, view the land, especially Jericho.' And they went and came into the house of a prostitute whose name was Rahab and lodged there" (Joshua 2:1).

Who is Rahab? A Canaanite woman living in Jericho, Rahab is a prostitute who is also a biblical heroine. A woman who was considered an outcast because of her profession. We all feel like an outcast at times. Rahab basically helps the spies that Joshua sent out to scope out the land before they took it. Jericho was a land promised to Joshua and his forefathers to possess the land. God promised them the land not because there were righteous but because of the wickedness of the Anakites. "The Lord has brought me here to take possession of this land because of my righteousness." No, it is on account of the wickedness of these nations that the Lord is going to drive them out before you. It is not because of your righteousness or your integrity that you are going in to take possession of their land; but on account of the wickedness of these nations, the Lord your God will drive them out before you, to accomplish what he swore to your fathers, to Abraham, Isaac, and Jacob. Understand, then, that it is not because of your righteousness that the Lord your God is giving you this good land to possess, for you are a stiff-necked people (Deuteronomy 9:4-6). People who have shown you wickedness, God is getting ready to hand them over and it's not because you speak in tongues with a might burning fire, it because He is tired of this wicked world.

Rahab was a woman who was head of her household. Many women today are head of household due to not being married. Rahab played a special part in Israel's presence in the land. When she hides the spies, she made a deal with them to secure her fate as well as her family's fate. She lets the spies know that she knows of their God and how he handled the Red Sea, therefore she feared what their God could do. She knew that God made something dry out of something wet, she knew her assignment and what side she should be on. In this season we must know our assignment and whose side to be on. If God tells you to hide then you hide, if He tells you to go then go. Rahab was a woman of faith, who served pagan gods. How can that be so? Well simply she knew God was powerful and what He could do. I understand that because, I know God is all powerful, and knowing and is everywhere but sometimes I miss the mark because of self will, self-desires.

Society assumed due to her choice of profession that she might die, an early death filled with shame. As women we have been counted out due to some of our choices. We have been told that we don't matter, or it's a man's world. We have been faced with many decisions to make ends meet to support our family. Just understand this my brothers and sisters if you will be willing and obedient you shall eat the good of the land (Isaiah 1:19). Some people might not believe but we have been building our homes just like the Proverbs 31 Woman, just because we don't build like them doesn't mean that you're not building. God will use you in your mess as long as you're willing to come of that mess. Just pay attention society will never go against their grain, bur God will every time. God didn't look at her as a harlot but someone He could use. The question at hand is how a woman of harlotry becomes a godly wife and mother in Israel. Where man counted her out, God worked in her favor because she was humble and had faith. Faith is what moves the hand of God, not circumstances, not hang-ups, not even people's view of who you are. God uses the most unlikely people to carry out his plan and his purpose.

Rahab was a woman who was not likely to make change or be a change agent in the Kingdom of God. People will look down on who because you act differently, talk different, eat different and live different, but God. She is considered a bad girl in the Bible, you have been told that you're a bad girl, not capable of doing anything good.

God turns Rahab's past into purpose, she was willing and ready to let go of what was. Trust me if God change me, He can change you. There's nothing too horrible about you or what you have done that God's love will not overtake. I had to stop allowing my past choices to determine my future blessings. I had to understand that Jesus died for all my sins, all my failures so that I could have a Joyful life. Just like God saw the best in you, you must see the best in you to move into your next. The enemy will tell you over and over again about your past, but I'm so glad I know Who holds my future. In this season God is about to test our faith for our purpose. We might have to do what Abram did and leave our comfortable place so that God can show us a land flowing with milk and honey. I trusted God for this very thing 23 years ago and He has not let me down. I made a lot of mistakes along the way, but I wouldn't take nothing for my journey now. Stop allowing what was changed to deter what shall be. What shall be is greatness, freedom, abundance. Your bold YES is what God is looking for. When you say YES, your YES will have a huge impact on you, your family, and the world. Your bad story will bring men and women to God. It will show them what God can and will do for other's when we say YES. Rahab said YES when she hides the spies and save her entire family and became part of the lineage of Jesus. God's faithfulness, His unconditional love and His promises were revealed in Rahab's life. He is the same God of yesterday and today and forever (Hebrews 13:8).

In the book of James, he tells us of how Rahab character can be converted by living faith and yields works (James 2:25). Now she is no longer called a harlot but rather the wife of Salmon, the mother of Boaz, and the ancestor of Jesus (Matthew 1:5-16). God says you will no longer be called no good, not enough, worthless but now you will be called overcomer, survivor, winner. It's all because of God's grace and mercy to change your mess to a message because of your faith. What I once was, I am not now. I am a new person, for the One who died once for me has given me a new name—daughter of the Messiah." (See Romans

6:10; 2 Corinthians 5:17; Revelation 2:17). So, I say arise daughter of Zion, you shall whatsoever you believe and desire.

Prayer: Our Father who art in heaven, hallowed be thy name. Thy kingdom come. Thy will be done on earth as it is in heaven. Give us this day our daily bread, and forgive us our trespasses, as we forgive those who trespass against us, and lead us not into temptation, but deliver us from evil. For thine is the kingdom and the power, and the glory, forever and ever. So, Lord here we are standing in the need of your grace, mercy and favor because we know that we have not done everything according to your instructions. Please forgive us, Create in us a clean heart and a contrite spirit. We are sorry that it took us this long to say Yes, but we now understand and believe that everything will work together for our good, because we love you and called according to your purpose.

Thank you for no condemnation because of our choices, thank you for holding us in the palm of your hand and your bosom. Thank you for reminding me that my past will not condemn me, that it will only push me to my destiny because of my faith. I decree and declare that No Weapon that is formed against me will be able to prosper. I decree and declare that I am more than a conqueror through Christ Jesus. Thank you for you unfailing love for me. Thank you for counting me in when others counted me out. Selah

Missionary Tamika Thomas

Tamika S. Thomas is the third born of five children to the late Superintendent Lon K. Thomas Sr. and the late Missionary Connie Thomas. She has a background in Social Work and graduated from Eastern New Mexico University 2007. Tamika has gained 20 years of experience working with different nonprofit organizations. Including developing innovative curriculum and teaching adult education at Goodwill, that serves people with barriers to employment populations. She managed the Boys unit at a youth shelter, where she supervised 6 staff and 25 children. Furthermore, she has worked on the college campus of Eastern New Mexico University in African American Affairs as an Assistant Director. Tamika also worked for two different afterschool programs for low-income families.

Tamika earned her certification of Life coach in the areas of Motivation & Christian in 2021. She is committed to God and winning souls for the kingdom. She is deeply devoted to improving the lives that she encounters. She provides team leadership, driven performance, program improvement and quality initiatives. Tamika is a visionary leader known for her ability to win community support and develop key relationships with a shared sense of purpose. This is Tamika Thomas better referred to as "Missionary "or "Mika T".

While in the Waiting Process: Believe the Word & Trust God.

Time is definitely an interesting thing. There are only 24 hours in a day, 1,440 minutes, 86,400 seconds. Yet some days seem never ending. Other days seem to fly right by. Depending on what is happening in our lives at the moment seems to also have an effect on how we see time. For instance, when we are on vacation those days appear to be short. But when we are dealing with troubling situations the expiration date seems not to exist. And in this life where we seemingly spend the majority of time is in a waiting process.

Think about it in order for children to come into the world the parent or parents must wait the standard 9 months. There are instances when the baby comes prematurely but there still is a waiting process. There are also instances where the baby isn't quite ready to come out and comes out later. No matter which of those situations is the outcome a waiting process must take place. Conception has to take place before the birth of a child.

So, there is a process that happens between conception and birth. I have yet to meet or read about children coming out of the womb crawling or walking or talking. Parents have to wait until the child develops different motor skills to be able to gain movement. The children don't start off automatically going to school again the parents have to wait until the child becomes of age to attend school. And then the parent has to wait and teach the child how to become an adult.

Oh, there are other areas in our lives where we have to wait. To name a few others, before you can eat any food you have to wait for it to be cooked or prepared. When you go to the doctor's office the majority of the visit is filled with waiting because the doctors are seeing other patients. Even when you drive around town there are times that you have to wait at the red light and at the stop sign. Sometimes you have to wait because there's an accident that happened or a funeral procession that is taking place. With all of these different examples of waiting that we have to do in life, one would think mankind would be experts at waiting. But that is not always the case.

Sarah

I want to take this time to interject a story of a woman who waited on a promise. This Promise was actually spoken to her husband before it was told to her. And it was a promise that would change her life forever. Sarai was the wife of Abram whose name was changed to Abraham by God. Abraham was promised to be the father of many nations and hold that he would have a baby boar by his wife Sarai whose name would be changed to Sarah, and she would become the mother of many nations.

In the 15th chapter of Genesis is where you can read how Abraham was promised an heir. Abraham and his wife were in a waiting process for their promise. In the sixteenth chapter Genesis you can read how Sarai had no children and took things into her own hands and offered the solution of Abraham bearing a child with her maid Hagar. If you review chapter 15 and 16 you will see how God made the promise to Abraham and how Sarai became impatient in the waiting process. And in her own way tried to help the promise come to fruition.

My brothers and my sisters while we are waiting on God, he does not need our help to get to the final outcome. What God needs us to do is to believe his word and trust Him. Sara moved ahead instead of waiting for what God said. Her actions caused her to go through trials and she treated people ugly. In the seventeenth chapter Abraham is reminded of what God Said in chapter 15. Below you will find the promise for Sarai.

Genesis 17:15-19 AMP

Then God said to Abraham, "As for Sarai your wife, you shall not call her name Sarai (my princess), but her name will be Sarah (Princess). I will bless her, and indeed I will also give you a son by her. Yes, I will bless her, and she shall be a mother of nations; kings of peoples will come from her." Then Abraham fell on his face and laughed, and said in his heart, "Shall a child be born to a man who is a hundred years old? And shall Sarah, who is ninety years old, bear a child?" And Abraham said to God, "Oh, that Ishmael [my firstborn] might live before You!" But God said, "No, Sarah your wife shall bear you a son indeed, and you shall name him Isaac (laughter); and I will establish My covenant with him for an everlasting covenant and with his descendants after him.

At times we have been promised things and they seem like they're never going to happen. In the 17th chapter of Genesis, we see God reassuring Abraham that what he said would come to pass. Believers never give up on what God says!

I wish that I could say after the passage of scripture that you just read in chapter 17 Sarah was fully convinced of what God was going to do. But in chapter 18 we find out that she laughs at what she hears God say. I want to remind us that God Specializes in situations that are impossible. Her laughter came because she was old according to her own admission. She couldn't believe that she would experience pleasure and delight because all this time she had been barren. At times we become so complacent with our situation and with the way things are that we don't believe change can come. So, we stop expecting the things that have been spoken to us by God. The next 5 verses from the 18th chapter of Genesis you can read where the promise was established again, and Sarah laughed.

Genesis 18:10-15 AMP

He said, "I will surely return to you at this time next year; and behold, Sarah your wife will have a son." And Sarah was listening at the tent door, which was behind him. Now Abraham and Sarah were old, well advanced in years; she was past [the age of] childbearing. So Sarah laughed to herself [when she heard the Lord's words], saying, "After I have become old, shall I have pleasure and delight, my Lord (husband) being also old?" And the Lord asked Abraham, "Why did Sarah laugh [to herself], saying, 'Shall I really give birth [to a child] when I am so old?' Is anything too difficult or too wonderful for the Lord? At the appointed time, when the season [for her delivery] comes, I will return to you and Sarah will have a son." Then Sarah denied it, saying, "I did not laugh"; because she was afraid. And He (the Lord) said, "No, but you did laugh."

When we have doubted God as Sarah did we must own up to what we have done. She didn't outwardly laugh, she just laughed within herself. It should tell you that God knows everything about us. He knows when we're right he knows when we're wrong. We have to learn to be filled with ourselves so we will be fair with God. Doubting is a part of this walk of faith. But when we doubt, we have to cry out to God and ask him to help our unbelief. In the 18th chapter of Genesis, we can read how God again reassured his people of the promise. It is not until the 21st chapter of Genesis where we see the Promise brought to fruition.

Genesis 21:1-3 AMP

The Lord graciously remembered and visited Sarah as He had said, and the Lord did for her as He had promised. So, Sarah conceived and gave birth to a son for Abraham in his old age, at the appointed time of which God had spoken to him. Abraham named his son Isaac (laughter), the son to whom Sarah gave birth.

In chapter 21 here we have just read that God manifested the promise. Three powerful words here Sarah gave birth. Those words solidified that it didn't matter what happened between chapters 15 and 21 God was true to his word. I am not saying that the things you go through in life are not important but what I am saying is that in the waiting process you're going to go through things in life. Our actions have consequences while we're waiting for the promise to be fulfilled. I want to encourage you not to take situations into your own hand. Because you may prolong the waiting.

One may ask what shall I do while I wait? I'm going to live life. I'm going to praise God. I'm going to trust and believe. We must also obey just what God says. Although life may seem trying and too hard to bear be encouraged and know that God is there. We have to carry our burdens and whatever we face to Him. He truly cares for in the things that concern us.

I hope you have found something within this Bible study to hold on to while you wait. Waiting is a process that we all experience but it's how we wait and what we do while we wait that could affect the outcome. Below you will find questions that may really help you gain some insight about yourself and about your relationship with God.

Reflection and Answer

1) Is there a specific promise that you feel like you're waiting on God to fulfill?

_____

_____

_____

_____

_____

2) How long have you waited for this promise? Do you still believe that the promise will happen?

_____
_____
_____
_____
_____

3) Do you find yourself doubting because of certain circumstances like Sarah?

_____
_____
_____
_____
_____

4) What are some nuggets that you have taken away from this lesson?

_____
_____
_____

5) Do you believe in God and will you trust his word?

BLUEPRINTS FROM HEAVEN-WOMEN IN THE BIBLE EDITION BOOK 2| 2022
DEVOTION & COLABORATION

Evangelist Priscilla Vargas

Evangelist Priscilla Vargas was born in California. She has two sons and seven grandchildren. She graduated from Lubbock High in 1989. She has a certification in cosmetology and is currently refreshing in nails. She also has her licensed in lash extension.

Ms. Vargas is an Evangelist and an inspirational singer. For 9 years she has been doing her outreach ministry that is called 'After God's own Heart'. She is also a licensed Christian Life Coach.

Jochebed: Mother of Faith and Courage in God

As we read about the woman, Jochebed, we see a mother of great faith and courage in God. Jochebed, was a daughter of Levi and the mother of Aaron, Moses, and Miriam. Jochebed gave birth to a son from her husband Amran that would be named Moses. Amran and Jochebed had the faith and fear of God therefore not allowing the Egyptians to kill their son as King Pharoah commanded to kill every newborn that was a boy.

King Pharoah observed that the Hebrew people were growing in numbers, and fearing that they might soon outnumber the Egyptians, therefore commanded the death of every male infant. Jochebed hid her son for three months until she could no longer hide him anymore. Therefore, she stepped out in faith and courage and placed him in a basket made of papyrus reeds and waterproofed it with tar and pitch. Jochebed lays the baby inside and lays it among the reeds along the bank of the Nile River.

The baby sister stood watching at a distance to see what would happen to him. Pharoah's daughter came to bathe in the river. As she was bathing, she saw a basket and had her maids bring it to her. The baby's sister approached the princess and said should I go and find one of the Hebrew women to nurse the baby for you? The princess replied, "Yes do!" The baby's sister then went and called the baby's mother, Jochebed. The princess tells Jochebed I will pay you for your help to take care of the baby and nurse him for me. Jochebed took him home and nursed him. Later when the baby grows up and becomes a boy, Jochebed returned him to the princess. The princess then adopts the little boy as her son and names him, Moses for she explained, "I lifted him out of the water."

Jochebed was a human being just as all of us are today. She had feelings just like you and me. She had hard problems to face just like you and I have. But in the midst of this trial, she had confidence and hope in God. Jochebed based her faith on the promises of God's word. Both Amran and Jochebed knew God had a special purpose for their child. The parents of Moses believed that God would preserve him and use him for His purpose.

Jochebed could not bear to see her baby perish in the river, but it was by faith and the love she had for baby to cast him in the river. It was by "faith" that he was hidden, not fear! Jochebed knew in her heart that God's promise of His word over Moses had to come to pass and she needed to go forth in faith and courage and let God's plan succeed!

"Relating my faith and love to God and for my sons like Jochebed"

As I read about Jochebed, the mother of Moses, it brought confirmation and knowing to my spirit of how my life of being a mother of my two sons relates to Jochebed and her story. My sons and I are all we have ever had and still do. We have been each other's strength, love, and hope for one another. As my sons grew up since they were babies, I had to protect, nourish and love them as both parents. Their father left when my oldest son was 1 year old, and my youngest son was not even born yet. It was an unexpected surprise to know that I would be a single mother with two sons, but God knew.

I have always been a God-fearing woman but had some hardships along the way. I always put my trust, faith, love, hope, and life in Jesus for I was raised up serving and knowing Jesus. As raising my two handsome sons I prayed and gave them to The Lord to have His way, impart in them a calling, and that they have a great and awesome plan and purpose in God.

I was put in a situation where I knew I had to protect my sons from harm and had to do whatever it took to protect them. One day as we were walking around at the flea market, I was approached by their father's mother. Mind you, she was not a very pleasant woman to speak and be around due to her heart being so bitter. When I was married to her son, my son's father, she was a very controlling and bitter person. Their father did not have a very good relationship with his mother, which was very sad. Eventually, their father and I got a divorce due to his cheating and wanting to continue to be out in the world. I knew that right there and then I had to be both parents to my two sons to give them both the love and guidance they needed.

Five years of being divorced from their father, he was shot and killed. I was then truly and literally the only parent my sons had left. I knew that God was and has been with me the whole time, but I truly needed God more than ever. I prayed and put myself and my sons in God's hands to let His will be done.

After my son's father's passing was when my son's grandmother tried to come in and control. She came up to me at the flea market and told me she was taking me to court for grandparents right where there she would convince the boys to live with her and call her momma. She told me that she had a dream that she won and hired the best lawyer in town. I told her that I did not have much money, but I will do whatever it takes to protect my sons! I told her I may not afford the best lawyer in town, but I will ask God to be My Defender! After this conversation, my sons overheard our conversation and they said, "Momma we don't want to go with her," and I said you will not have to if you don't want to because we are going to pray to Jesus to protect us and help us." They said, "Okay."

As we went to court, I prayed to God telling Him I am going before a really bitter person that has lots of money. but I know that my God is greater and will make the impossible possible for my sons and me. During the process of going to court, my son's aunt came to me and said I heard that my mother wants to take you to court. I said yes. She said, "Well I want to help you because I do not want my nephews around her due to her attitude and character." I knew by having faith and courage in God that God made a way when there seemed no way and had their aunt testify on my behalf. Hallelujah!! You know that was the hand and favor of God placed in our life. The judge voted in our behalf, and I won the case! Glory to God!

I saw my sons' eyes full of joy, relief, and happiness that mom had protected them. I knew that God would provide! When God has a plan and purpose in your life, it will be fulfilled no matter what obstacles and schemes come your way! We have to learn to follow and trust in Jesus in all areas of our life. We have to focus and step out in faith at times even when it doesn't seem possible. I still pray for their grandmother for a transformed healed and restored heart.

There are so many times that God lets us know that we must step out in courage and faith. He sends The Holy Spirit to lead us, direct us and warn us. I have seen God show up and show out in my life. Let's be encouraged and walk in the footsteps and example of Jochebed that walked in faith, love, and courage. Jochebed applied the word of God over her and her children and stood on a firm foundation that she would be sensitive to The Holy Spirit to be led to lead her family no matter what she faced ahead.

God will always fight for us in our behalf when we remain faithful and obedient in His word and love. This is the love of a mother, making great sacrifices and being willing to do the difficult things that parenting requires. As God quietly worked in Jochebed's life, be assured that He is working behind the scenes in your life as well.

Reflection and Answer

1. Considering the circumstances, do you think it took courage to come against Pharoah?

BLUEPRINTS FROM HEAVEN-WOMEN IN THE BIBLE EDITION BOOK 2| 2022
DEVOTION & COLABORATION

_____

_____

_____

_____

_____

_____

2. Does Jochebed display courage and faith? How?

_____

_____

_____

_____

_____

3. List ways Jochebed displayed her faith and courage in this circumstance?

_____

_____

_____

_____

_____

4. What and/or who does Jochebed draw her courage from?

5. She needed a plan to save her son's life. What was that?

6. Who was the one that was on the watch out while Jochebed laid the baby in the basket in The Nile River? What was the name?

7. What did she use to build that basket for her baby?

8. What ways do you see God working in Jochebed's behalf?

9. What was the parents' name?

10. What was the name the princess of Egypt named the baby and what did it stand for?

_____

_____

_____

_____

_____

_____

Prayer of Encouragement

I come to Lord on behalf of my beautiful sisters in faith asking that you fill us and overflow us with your love, unspeakable joy, and understanding. Lord instill in us the wisdom of Jochebed, the strong faith, amazing love, and the direction of The Holy Spirit to walk in the amazing, strong faith and courage for our children. We come to you right now in faith and in agreement that as each day goes by that you continue to be with us letting us feel your blessed assurance that you are beside us. As we walk this life's journey and make our decisions for ourselves and for our family, we pray right now that The Lord's will be done, and The Holy Spirit be our Helper.

We impart in each of us the supernatural faith, strength, courage, joy, understanding, and love to keep trusting in you, Jesus! We place our children in your hands believing that you have a great and prosperous plan for their lives. We thank you Jesus for your unfailing love, mercy, and grace toward us and our children. We believe and trust in faith that you will always see us through, and the hedge of protection is over our children always. We will walk in the faith and courage of Jochebed for our children and for the love we have for you, Jesus! We believe that as we pray that you have our every step, our every breath, our every circumstance for us and our children and will always see us through! Your word never comes back to void so we will hold onto the promises of the word of God as tablets in our hearts. We receive and believe that all is well, all is done, and all shall come to pass of your perfect plan and purpose in Jesus' name. Amen

Encouraging Verses:

Isaiah 41:10-So do not fear, for I am with you; do not be dismayed, for I am your God. I will strengthen you and help you; I will uphold you with my righteous right hand.

John 16:33-In the world you will have tribulation. But take heart; I have overcome the world.

Philippians 4:6-7-Do not be anxious about anything, but in every situation, by prayer and petition, with thanksgiving, present your requests to God. And the peace of God, which transcends all understanding, will guard your hearts and your minds in Christ Jesus.

Romans 8:28-We know that for those who love God all things work together for good, for those who are called according to His purpose.

Romans 15:13-May the God of hope fill you with all joy and peace as you trust in Him, so that you may overflow with hope by the power of The Holy Spirit.

BLUEPRINTS FROM HEAVEN-WOMEN IN THE BIBLE EDITION BOOK 2| 2022
DEVOTION & COLABORATION

Minister Barbara Slater

Dr. Barbara Slater is a native Floridian that received the commission to minister to the oppressed, preach the Gospel, Heal the brokenhearted, and proclaim deliverance to the captives. God has given her a heart for the women, teens, and children. Molested as a child, became a runaway teen, homeless veteran and a former drug and alcohol abuser. The men in her life were verbally and physically abusing her. Dr. Slater has been delivered from the spirit of suicide and truly has the heart for the hurting. While operating in the gifts of the Spirit, she ministers to the body with love from the East to West. She is currently on assignment to the Nation. She is dressed in the full armor of God and used her military background to do battle for God's people with strategic warfare.

Throughout complex trials, extended tests, crooked roads and the school of hard knocks, God birthed Touch & Agree Women's Ministry. While she experienced pain and suffering personally by allowing her to identify with hurting women all over the country with opening shelters for those that seek refuge. She aids them by offering housing, education, counseling, and support. The ministry offers conferences & seminars. Traveling through the country, she is using that which was meant for harm to help others. Dr. Slater is currently establishing a retreat center for Women in Hawaii.

Athaliah

What do we learn today about Athaliah?

Athaliah was the daughter of Jezebel. The wicked queen evil Jezebel is termed spiritually as a murdering spirit killing of the anointing the prophetic. I read an outline by Jennifer LeClaire about the wicked queen and as I studied the spiritual perspective of the law and what it means today.

Jezebel was her mother, and she was a wicked queen. Jezebel who was a Phoenician wife of King Ahab. I am not sure was it known if she was the daughter or stepdaughter, who according to the counts in second kings they press the idolatry on Israelites kingdom, who was finally killed per Elijah's prophecy. The Jezebel spirit term is often used to describe someone who is conniving and seductive. It used on churches and marriages. The Jezebel spirit is sinister. The Spirit, focuses on the prophetic mantle seeking to kill, steal a ministry, a home, and a marriage. Jezebel uses subjection to wall either a man or a married man a woman of the cloth, utterly destroying or desecrating their life and the anointing and if not just kill them, Jezebel.

So that leads us to understand that Athaliah is the daughter of Jezebel with the spirit Athaliah, of not only a Jezebel spirit but has a spirit of vengeance she not only comes wipe out the ministry or destroy a husband, a man of God or a wife, a woman of God but she comes to wipe out the entire genealogy of your family because it's a spirit of retaliation with a vengeance.

Athaliah has been dormant. She is deadly, at the death of her mother and father the king of Israel. Scripture says after the death of her family she killed the entire family she's search the throne and reigns for seven years and then she massacres all the family members of the Royal house except Joel second king 11 verses 13. You can't spiritually fight Jezebel without being ready to take on the spirit of Athaliah which is revenge and retaliation. Athaliah is a vengeful spirit, the spirit of being dormant, during the ministry of John the Baptist. Herodotus and she set her daughter Salome to dance and request the head of John the Baptist, because she married the brother of a husband and John the Baptist call them out.

What she did was go get Salome which is the spirit to literally dance before her room and get what she wanted. She danced so seductively that he asked her what she wanted and she came up and whispered in his ear, "I want the head of John the Baptist St." John the Baptist was a type of Elijah so it was coming again around.

We today have to be so careful to not only take heed to what is going on in the world today that we not only do we have a Jezebel spirit to fight, but we have to be on God all focus to be able to fight the spirit of Athaliah, because if not it will come and try to destroy the whole genealogy of your family.

Today we've been dealing with spirit of Jezebel but when we begin to look in our young men and women or boys and girls our children are dying because we as a church are failing to deal with the spirit of Athaliah. I come to let you know that once you know and see the spirit, we're going to pray that every demonic strong hole that has come against your family will be destroyed. We are going to pray that we destroy the spirit of Jezebel and spirit of Athaliah, which is retaliation because we will break degeneration of curse over our children and families of our home and over our nation.

Athaliah was the daughter of King Ahab and Queen Jezebel of Israel, the Queen consort of Judah as the wife of King Jehoram, a descendant of King David, and later queen regnant c. 841–835 BCE. (Wikipedia

Born: 898 BC, Sebastia

Died: 836 BC, Jerusalem

Spouse: Jehoram

Children: Ahaziah of Judah

Parents: Ahab, Jezebel

Grandchild: Jehoash of Judah

Siblings: Jehoram of Israel, Ahaziah of Israel

Queen Athaliah is the only woman in the Hebrew Bible that reportedly reigned as a monarch within Israel/Judah. After her son's brief rule, she killed the remaining dynasty members and commanded for six years when she was overthrown. She is the daughter of either Omri, king of Israel (2 Kgs 8:26; 2 Chr 22:2), or, more probably, of his son King Ahab (2 Kgs 8:18; 2 Chr 21:6; the Jewish historian Josephus cites this in Antiquities), who ruled from 873 to 852 B.C.E. There is no evidence that she was the daughter of Ahab's chief wife, Jezebel. Athaliah married Jehoram (reigned 851–843 B.C.E.) of Judah (2 Kgs 8:18; 2 Chr 21:6). After Jehoram's death, their son Ahaziah reigned for one year, and "his mother was his counselor in doing wickedly" (2 Chr 22:3).

After Ahaziah is killed in a dynastic struggle (2 Kings 9), Athaliah sets out to kill the rest of the royal dynasty and seizes the throne of Judah in Jerusalem (2 Kings 9; 2 Chr 22:10–23:21). She remains the sole monarch for six years (842–836 B.C.E.). In the seventh year, a revolution led by Jehoiada, the priest puts on the throne the seven-year-old Joash, Ahaziah's child, rescued by his paternal aunt (and Jehoiada's wife) Jehosheba from the royal bloodbath six years earlier. The overthrow takes place in the Jerusalem temple. Athaliah is killed in what she terms "treason" (2 Kgs 11:14: 2 Chr 23:13) against her reign.

The biblical evaluation of her rule is negative. Both 2 Kings 11 and 1 Chronicles (especially chap. 24) connect Athaliah with Baal worship, even though her name contains the theophoric element yah[u] (yhwh), like the names of other figures in the story. The priestly objection to her could also be motivated by hatred for a non-Davidic ruler and, particularly, a woman ruler. However, that she managed to sustain her Reign for six years can be attributed to her successful use of various sources of power: her royal origins and connections, involvement in her husband's and son's reigns, economic independence, personal ability, and political knowledge—all of which are not mentioned, apart from notes on her evil influence on her husband and son.

Reflection and Answer

Do you have an Athaliah in your life that is holding you back from obtaining what God has for you? If so, who or what is that?

_____
_____
_____
_____

How can you overcome the spirit of an Athaliah?

_____
_____
_____
_____

Dr. Dianah Kamande

Dianah Kamande is a Kenyan widows' rights activist who is a survivor of Gender-Based violence who became a young widow in 2013. Her experience motivated her towards the founding of Come Together Widows and Orphans Organization and Association of Survivors of Gender-Based-Violence, both of which are based in Kenya. She believes in the words of the Former UN Secretary General Ban Ki Moon "No woman should lose her status, livelihood or property when her husband dies". She is a motivational speaker and a mentor to many.

Dianah is a mother of two girls. She is also an author of the book Scars of Honor.

ACADEMIC QUALIFICATIONS:

- Diploma in Governance and Women in Leadership in Africa- University of Nairobi.
- Bachelor's degree in Governance, Peace and Conflict Studies- African Nazarene University.
- Masters in Cases in Gender Equality-European Business University Luxembourg (2021-2023)

BOARD MEMBER

Dianah is a board member at Anti-Female Mutilation Board, a board which is a Kenyan government body responsible for implementing the

Prohibition of FGM Act.

AWARDS

Her passion to advocate, inspire and empower widows in Kenya has earned her recognition both locally (in Kenya) and internationally.

- Trail Blazers Presidential Award on 8th March 2022 during the International Women's Day

- Head of State Commendation

In recognition of her exemplary contribution to making widows matter in Kenya, she was honored and feted with a Head of State Commendation (H.S.C) by the President of the Republic of Kenya on 12th December 2018.

- Unwavering Advocacy Award

This award was given to her by Ms. Heather Ibrahim-Leather the Founder and President of Global Fund for Widows for relentless service in widows work in and out of Kenya.

- Above and Beyond

This award was given to her by United Widows in South Carolina in honor of the exemplary leadership she offered.

- On 19th November 2020, she was recognized as one of the distinguished keynote speakers at the 2020 Global Women Empowerment Summit organized by the Prodigy Bureau Global.

She has also Earned the following Awards:

- Individual Empowering Grassroots Women Award by Women on Boards Network
- Global Women Empowerment Summit Award -Dubai
- Women in Wellness Technology Fashion Award -Dubai
- The Spirit of Philanthropy Individual Award
- Exemplary Services of Special Interest Groups Award by National Gender and Equality Commission-Kenya
- Zuri Award Humanitarian Honoree by Go Gaga Experiential
- Global Change Maker Award by Ladies of all nations international UK
- Beautiful Survivors of the World Award- Ladies of All Nations International UK
- Honorary Doctorate in Humanitarianism from United Kingdom
- Top Women in Business Award 2019 Lifetime Achievement Award
- Queens Ministry Boston at Extra Mile Award
- Global Goodwill Ambassador Humanitarian Award

• Women in Africa Heroes Award among many others

Dianah has been an exceptional leader for the widows in Kenya to the extent that she has been found fit to represent widows in international fora like the Commission on the Status of Women (CSW) 62 and 63 in New York. Through her efforts Kenyan Government has put widows in their workplan. The widows in Kenya have benefitted a lot from her proactiveness, courage and resilience. She has ensured that the relevant stakeholders are always aware of the plight of widows in Kenya and is making sure that widows' dignity is being restored.

Dianah Kamande HSC has trained so many widows to become paralegals and can represent themselves in court. This is her pride seeing Women who were once despised standing in court and reclaiming what is rightfully theirs. Seeing Women who have been silent about Gender Based Violence coming out to speak about it and condemn it. Dianah Kamande HSC has started vocational Training institutes to Empower Women with knowledge and power. Seeing women able to transact their mobile money without being oppressed and being denied what is rightfully theirs has given her a lot of joy.

JEZEBEL

Jezebel was the daughter of Ithobaal I of Tyre and the wife of Ahab, King of Israel, according to the Book of Kings of the Hebrew Bible. According to the biblical narrative, Jezebel, along with her husband, instituted the worship of Baal and Asherah on a nationwide and according to the Bible (Kings I and II), she provoked conflict that weakened Israel for decades by interfering with the exclusive worship of the Hebrew God also known as Yahweh, disregarding the rights of the common man, and defying the great prophets Elijah and Elisha.

After her marriage to King Ahab, Jezebel emerges as the power behind the throne. Their union represents a political alliance, bringing advantages to both nations. It is also an opportunity for Jezebel to foster the spread of her Baal religion with its many gods, ritual sex, and temple prostitutes. She hates the monotheistic Hebrew religion, and when she becomes queen, Israelites have already begun worshiping alien idols. Under his wife's malevolent influence, King Ahab protects and encourages pagan rituals, prompting Yahweh to inflict a three-year drought in a land where people are spurning him. Seizing the initiative, Jezebel imports 450 priests of Baal from her native Phoenicia and has many of Yahweh's prophets murdered.

To Jews, Baal worship was the worst sin against God. To settle the question of who was supreme? Either Yahweh or Baal. The prophet Elijah devises a contest on Mount Carmel. Whichever side can set afire and destroy a sacrificial bull by divine intervention will be acknowledged as the true God. A whole day,

Jezebel's 450 prophets performed a hopping dance about the altar, at times mutilating themselves with lances and swords. Nothing happens. Then it is Elijah's turn to pray, and the response is immediate. "Fire from the Lord descended and consumed the burnt offering, the wood, the stones, and the earth. When they saw this, all the people flung themselves on their faces and cried out: 'The Lord alone is God.

Elijah then slaughters the pagan prophets—revenge for Jezebel's murder of Yahweh's followers—and the Hebrew God rewards him by ending Israel's drought. The die is now cast between the triumphant prophet and the humiliated queen. After her followers are killed, she sends a venomous message to Elijah threatening his destruction, prompting him to flee to safety.

JEZEBELS DRAMA IN THE PALACE

Jezebel's husband covets a vineyard owned by Naboth that he wants for a garden. Naboth's refusal to sell his family inheritance sends Ahab into a funk. Jezebel asserts her dominance. "Now is the time to show yourself king over Israel," she says scornfully. "I will get the vineyard of Naboth the Jezreelite for you."

How she succeeds reinforces the eternal image of Jezebel as a scheming, murderous vixen. Forging the king's signature, she sends letters to townspeople falsely accusing Naboth of blaspheming God. When Naboth is publicly confronted, Jezebel urges the crowd: "Then take him out, and stone him to death." Naboth dies, and his property reverts to the royal family.

Jezebel's nefarious plot succeeds, but the inexorable denouement swiftly follows. Yahweh summons his prophet Elijah and instructs him to tell King Ahab that he will be punished. "Say to him: 'Would you murder and take possession? In the very place where the dogs lapped up Naboth's blood, the dogs will lap up your blood, too.' " Elijah dutifully relates Yahweh's prophecy to the king but predicts that Jezebel, not her husband will be torn apart and eaten by dogs.

What is Jezebel remembered for?

1. Most of the prophets of Yahweh were killed at her command.

2. When Jezebel married King Ahab of Israel (ruled c. 874–853 BCE), she persuaded him to introduce the worship of the Tyrian god Baal-Melkart, a nature god.

3. Manipulation and seduction, she misled the saints of God into sins of idolatry and sexual immorality.

4. Jezebel was a Phoenician princess in the 9th century who married Ahab, the prince of Israel.

5. A woman who is regarded as evil and scheming.

Was JEZEBEL a Virtuous Woman at all? I don't think so because she cannot be compared to the Noble woman of Proverbs 31. She swallowed her husband in her thoughts because he was over controlling.

Reflection and Answer

What are your thoughts on how a virtuous woman should act?

_____
_____
_____
_____

What is Jezebel known for?

_____
_____
_____
_____

Sister Margo Williams

` Prophetess Margo Williams is the author of " When God Speaks, Poems and Prayers," I Am Divinely Designed," I Am that Butterfly, the Transformed Life," and other writings. She is known for her love of writing, photography, Advocacy/Education of Domestic Violence, Rape Crisis Intervention, Coaching and Public Speaking.

As a Prophetess, Margo's mission is to be effective in every God given assignment. She desires to see every individual she cross paths with, to know God and His purpose for their lives.

Margo works in the field of Psychology/Human Services as an Interventionist in educational settings with youth. She has worked in her field, with many communities for over 20 years, and has gained experience working with at-risk youth in foster care, Autistic/Blind individuals, teen-parents, and as a Behavior Interventionist.

The Woman at the Well

In the book of John 4, verses 1-42, you'll find the "Woman at the Well," experience. This woman went to draw water alone, not knowing that she'd end up having a life-changing encounter with Jesus. We don't know her name but do know she lived in a time when women were disregarded.

Jesus would travel through Samaria heading to Galilee. As He traveled, the city of Sychar is where Jesus would stop around 12 noon. This is also where Jacob's Well was located. His disciples were gone to the city to buy meat. Jesus was tired from traveling on His journey, and while resting there, a Samaritan woman would come to draw water. Jesus then asked the woman "Give me a drink (John 4:7)."

The woman replied to Jesus in John 4:9 NIV: 9) "You are a Jew, and I am a Samaritan woman. How can you ask me for a drink?" (For Jews do not associate with Samaritans.) John 4:9 NIV

Jesus answered the Samaritan woman in John 4:10 KJV: 10) "If thou knewest the gift of God, and who it is that saith to thee, give me to drink; thou wouldest have asked of him, and he would have given thee living water."

In John 4:11-12, the Samaritan woman also noticed that Jesus had no cup to draw water with, and told him the well was deep, which lets us know that she was very observant. She began to Inquire about this "living water," and if He was greater than Jacob.

Jesus responds in John 4:13-14 KJV: *13) Whosoever drinketh of this water shall thirst again: 14) But Whosoever drinkest of the water that I shall give*

him shall never thirst: but the water that I shall give him shall be in him a well of water springing up into everlasting life.

The Samaritan woman responded to Jesus in verse 15: *15) Sir, give me this water, that I thirst not, neither hither to draw.*

Jesus responds to the woman in verse 16: *16) Go, call thy husband, and hither back.*

This conversation opened the opportunity to discuss the woman's husband situation. She's had five husbands and was with a man who wasn't married to her. In John 4:17-18, is where this conversation takes place.

The Samaritan woman comes to the conclusion that Jesus was a prophet and began a dialogue in regard to worship in John 4:19-24. She then stated in (vs. 25), "I know the Messiah as cometh, which is called Christ: when he is come, he will tell us all things."

Jesus responded in John 4:26: *26) "I that speak unto thee am he"*

The disciples returned as Jesus was conversating with the woman. She then left her water jar and ran off to tell the people to "come, see a man which told me all things that ever I did: is not this the Christ?" There was excitement, because of what she testified. The Samaritans experienced Jesus for two days and many more became believers (John 4:27-41).

The Samaritans said to the woman in John 4:42: *42) Now we believe, not because of thy saying: for we have heard him for ourselves, and know that this is indeed the Christ, the Savior of the world.*

It wasn't by coincidence that the woman would go alone to Jacobs Well around the time Jesus was there. He knew the right time to show up and speak. This is the same thing for each of us. He knows when and where to meet you, and for many, it is at your lowest point. Jesus being a Jew, and still taking time to talk to her was evidence of His love for the world. He didn't follow the traditions of man, and didn't care about gender, or marital status. There was a sincere love for everyone.

The Samaritan woman was offered the living water, that only through salvation is given. She saw that she was finally accepted, unlike her experience living as a Samaritan. What we see is a new beginning, of finding individual purpose. As she would go and share her testimony, others would listen to her and have the same opportunity to experience newness. Knowing that she was forgiven, and never having to look back on the past was refreshing and life changing. Below are some scriptures that reference the living water:

Psalm 145:16 KJV reads: *16) Thou open thy hand and satisfy the desire of every living thing.*

Isaiah 12:3 KJV reads: *3) Therefore with joy shall ye draw water out of the wells of salvation.*

Isaiah 44:3 KJV reads: *3) For I will pour water upon him that is thirsty, and floods upon the dry ground; I will pour my spirit upon my seed, and my blessing upon thine offspring.*

John 7:38 KJV reads: *38) He that believeth on me, as the scripture hath said, out of his belly shall flow rivers of living water.*

This very Living Water Offered to the Woman at the Well, brought a renewed mind to her way of thinking. Although she's had five husbands, and the one she was with wasn't a husband, Jesus had given her much grace and mercy. She was still needed as a vessel to spread the good news and had a great purpose. Those around were able to look and see how only God can transform the lives of the lost and broken. Access is available to all who desire to have a personal relationship with our precious Heavenly Father.

My Life in Comparison

As I look at what we know about the Woman at the Well, I noticed that there was an issue with her identity. She was not the most popular person, was never called by a name, and didn't know where she fit in. She was judged harshly in the times that she lived and did not make the best choices when it came to men. She was a loner, in search of something more from life. It didn't seem as though she had the greatest support system, which made her the perfect candidate to be used.

I was so lost in my younger years and made terrible choices when it came to men. My choices opened me up to being a victim of different types of abuse. I did not love myself, and my self-esteem was stripped. Looking for love, in all the wrong places would leave me very bitter, and unable to trust anyone. I was judged harshly because the circumstances I had to deal with. When the Lord revealed Himself to me, I was still trying to figure myself out. I had an actual name in the natural, but spiritually, it had not been discovered.

As much as I tried to find where I fit in, I was ignored, which was necessary in my process. I would eventually learn of who I was in Christ and the reason I'm still breathing. It wasn't coincidental that I went through the many trials, because all of it was needed to strengthen me as I'm now being used as a vessel. Once we come into our Identity, we can then truly walk in the fullness of God's Will for our lives. There is then a sense of peace, and joy that you will experience, regardless of what we see in the world.

Reflection and Answer

1) How did Jesus show mercy to the Woman at the Well?

BLUEPRINTS FROM HEAVEN-WOMEN IN THE BIBLE EDITION BOOK 2| 2022
DEVOTION & COLABORATION

2) How did Jesus bring restoration to the Woman at the Well's life?

3) What part of the conversation between Jesus and the woman made her believe?

4) How does your life relate to the Woman at the Well?

BLUEPRINTS FROM HEAVEN-WOMEN IN THE BIBLE EDITION BOOK 2| 2022
DEVOTION & COLABORATION

_____

_____

_____

_____

_____

_____

5) In knowing the Woman at the Well's background, does it help you have more compassion for others? If so, how? How can you relate it to situations of today?

_____

_____

_____

_____

_____

6) What lesson did you learn from the dialogue between Jesus, and the Woman at the Well"?

_____

_____

_____

BLUEPRINTS FROM HEAVEN-WOMEN IN THE BIBLE EDITION BOOK 2| 2022
DEVOTION & COLABORATION

_____

7) What did God reveal to you, about Him?

8) What did the Woman say to Jesus regarding drawing water, and what does it mean to you?

9) Please share your thoughts about the "Living Water".

10) Do you know your Identity? Please, explain.

_____

_____

_____

_____

Prayer: Father, give each reader a visitation, so they may experience you on a supernatural level. Illuminate the readers' minds like never before, as they read, and meditate on Your Word. Let each person desire to know You more deeply, and not miss what You've called for them to do. Speak to them, in dreams and visions, that they may know Your voice. Let joy and Peace follow each reader. In Jesus's Name, Amen.

Sister Chantell Stubblefield-Bagley

Chantell is 53 years young. She graduated from Dunbar-Struggs High School in 1987 with honors. After graduating from high school, Chantell went on to attend Texas Tech University where she majored in Music Education. Chantell was a member of the Texas Tech Ensemble Choir, the marching band, and continued her voice training lessons which helped her to grow more as a singer and musician.

Chantell has worked with many different churches, choirs, praise teams, and musicians over the past 35 years, but she enjoyed, and grew the most with her church family at Full Armor Ministries, where she served as a Praise Team Member, and Praise and Worship Leader for several years.

Chantell is a very compassionate person who loves to help people whenever she can and in any way that she can. That's why Chantell is so grateful for the opportunity to work in the Financial Services Ministry of Covenant/Providence Healthcare System. In her position there, she is able to help people in ways that she never thought was possible and she can spread The Word of The Lord at the same time. Her prayer is always, "Lord help me to be a light to ALL I encounter today and everyday".

Chantell is married to the love of her life, Min. Willis E Bagley Sr. who grew up right here in Lubbock, Tx and who is also a graduate of the great Dunber-Struggs High School. Willis and Chantell have been married for 13 years. The Bagley's have four children and four grandchildren.

The Lord has tremendously blessed Chantell and her family and her prayer is that the Lord will continue to do so now and in the future.

The Story of Hannah

Summary

Allow me to introduce you to Hanna, a young beautiful woman that was stricken with barrenness. Her life was very difficult because she was unable to give her husband any children, which was publicly viewed as sin or a curse from God on the childless woman.

She was married to a certain man from the mountains of Ephraim, the hill country primarily occupied by the tribe of Ephraim. His name was Elkanah, which in Hebrew means "God has Created". Elkanah had two wives, the name of the one was Hannah, and the name of the other was Peninnah. Elkanah was married to Hannah first, and after being married for about ten years, he saw that Hannah bore him no children, so he took his second wife, Peninnah.

Elkanah and his family went to Shiloh, the religious center for the nation at this time, yearly to worship and sacrifice to the Lord of hosts. The Law demanded that the men of Israel appear before God on three festival occasions. Many brought their families with them, but it was not required. The fact that Hannah went with Elkanah yearly, showed her devotion to the Lord in that she also made annual treks to Shiloh to worship God. And when it came time for Elkanah to make an offering, he would give portions to Peninnah and to all of her sons and daughters, but he would give a double portion to Hannah, for he loved her although the Lord had closed her womb. This was a degrading and humiliating condition for a woman of the ancient Middle East.

So, for a Hebrew wife or concubine to be barren it was essentially viewed as disobedience to God, and the consequence was very public. And her rival, Peninnah who took every occasion to flaunt her children before Hannah, and would provoke her severely, to make her miserable. Peninnah would take ordinary everyday activities and use them like daggers against Hannah, by reminding her, at all hours of the day, of the difference between them.

Hannah wept bitterly and did not eat because Peninnah's constant taunting drove Hannah to depression. Hannah would not eat or drink even during mealtimes at Shiloh because the shame, and bitter anguish that she felt as a result of not having children weighed very heavily on her heart and in her soul. Peninnah knew that although she had given Elkanah children, she knew that Hannah was Elkanah's beloved, but nevertheless sought to gain some recognition from Elkanah, either in their home or in public.

While Peninnah taunted and harassed Hannah, Elkanah tried to encourage her. He would ask Hannah, "why are you so sad, and why do you not eat or drink?" (**1 Sam. 1:8**) Hannah was so distraught and tortured in her soul, that she wouldn't eat with the family while at Shiloh, and this continued year after year. She waited for them to finish eating, and then she arose and went before the Lord, to plead her case.

I can imagine in my mind, that Hannah went up to the alter, and began to pray and weep bitterly as she poured her soul out to the Father to remove this reproach from her soul and from her life. The constant harassment from Peninnah, and the public shaming and the torment of watching other women and wives with their children and being made to feel like that she was less than a woman because she couldn't give her husband children; it had all become too much for her to continue to bare. She was emotionally debilitated!!

Now the high priest at the time Eli, as he was seated in his judicial chair at the doorpost of the tabernacle, saw Hannah's lips moving but he could not hear any sound coming from her mouth. From that distance, Eli was unable to understand what Hannah was saying, but because of the long time she spent in prayer, Eli assumed that she was drunk and confronted her saying that she should put away her wine. Yes, her facial expressions and posture changed, and the tears were flowing down her face, and this is when she made her vow to the Lord! Hannah vowed that if God would give her a son, the child would be given back to God, and Hannah promised that her son would be a Nazarite for life.

Hannah respectfully answered Eli, immediately explaining that she had neither wine nor strong drink but that she was a woman of sorrowful spirit. She further explained that she was not a "wicked woman" without value, but that she has prayed to the Lord out of the abundance of her complaint and grief. That's when Eli then realized that he had misjudged her and he blessed her saying, "Go in peace, and the God of Israel grant your petition which you have asked of Him!" Hannah went her way and ate, and she was no longer sad.

So, the family rose early the next morning, worshiped before the Lord and returned home. Elkanah knew his wife and the Lord remembered her, and Hannah conceived and bore a son. When the child was weaned at about 3 years old, Hannah kept her vow to the Lord and gave him back to God.

How I relate to Hannah's story

I understand Hannah's plight because I too have had to deal with childlessness. I tried for years to have children when I was younger, but my attempts only turned to loss and disappointment. At first, conceiving was not the problem because I was able to conceive but carrying the baby to full term was the problem. I have given birth to two boys, (their names are Zacchaeus and Azariah by the way,) but unfortunately, they both were born prematurely, and they did not live. They were far enough along to where we had to have a funeral each time, and the pain and anguish of having to bury two baby boys in my lifetime was to much for me to handle. You place in the ground all of your hopes and dreams that you had for that child and also for yourself as a mother when that child goes into the ground. The pain of that moment is not something that I would wish on anyone.

Standing by year after year seeing girls' way too young to be a mother have children, drug addicts, girls/woman having abortions, and people who abuse children continue to have them, and yet there I was left empty handed. It was extremely difficult to understand why they were granted over and over again, the one thing in life that continued to elude me. Some of the things that people would say to me during that time, even though they were trying to help, it only made me feel worse and made me feel so hurt and inadequate. I had to lay before the Lord for years in order to be healed and to release the pain of not being the only thing that I ever wanted to be in this life......... a mother.

Even in the days that we live in now, people will try to make you feel like there's something wrong with you if you don't have any children. I had to allow the Father to heal my heart, my hurt and my self-esteem. It was a long and painful process, but I am still here and blessed to have been a mother figure to so many precious individuals over the years. I have actually raised more children than most parents, but they all belonged to someone else. Most of these children have stayed in contact with me over the years, and some of them are adults now, married and have children of their own and yes, I do take some satisfaction in knowing that I was instrumental in their lives and helping them to get to where they are now, and to become the people that they are today!

Reflection and Answer

1. Where was Hannah's husband, Elkanah from?

_____

_____

_____

BLUEPRINTS FROM HEAVEN-WOMEN IN THE BIBLE EDITION BOOK 2| 2022
DEVOTION & COLABORATION

2. What was Hannah stricken with?

3. What was the name of Elkanah's second wife?

4. Why did Elkanah take a second wife?

**BLUEPRINTS FROM HEAVEN-WOMEN IN THE BIBLE EDITION BOOK 2| 2022
DEVOTION & COLABORATION**

5. What was the name of the religious center for the nation at that time?

_____

_____

_____

_____

6. Who did Elkanah love the most of his two wives?

_____

_____

_____

_____

7. After going up to Shiloh, what did Hannah do after their worship feast?

_____

_____

_____

_____

8. What was Hannah's vow to the Lord if he gave her a son, and what

would he be for life?

_____

_____

_____

_____

9. What did the high priest Eli, think was wrong with Hannah after he observed her in prayer?

_____

_____

_____

_____

10. How old was Samuel when Hannah took him to the temple to dedicate him to the Lord?

_____

_____

_____

_____

PRAYER FOR THE READER

Dear heavenly Father, I first want to say thank you!!!! Thank you for your desire and will to heal all of my sisters that are in pain for one reason or another. Father God, please touch and heal ALL of the pain of every woman that has suffered the pain of losing a child, or not being able to conceive a child. Touch, heal and deliver my sisters of any stigma or labels that have been placed on them by people because they do not have children. Even if it's by choice, the world tries to make us think that it's something wrong with a woman that does not have children, but let my sisters know who they are in You Father, and please reveal to them their true worth, which is in you. And Father for every mother that carries the weight of her children on her shoulders, give her the strength, courage, and wisdom to lead her children in the way that you would have them to go.

Now Father, I pray a special prayer of blessing over each and every sister that is reading this prayer, whether she is a mother or not! Be strong my sister, take all of your hurt and pain to the Father. Wait for an answer, and then come out of your problem or trial bigger, better, and stronger than you were when you went in. I seal this prayer by the precious Holy Spirit of God and declare that it is so in the mighty name of our Lord and Savior Jesus Christ..........Amen.......and Amen!!!!!

Coach Liza Velasquez

Coach Liza A. Velasquez is a certified Christian counselor, empowerment coach, and a motivation speaker. She has decades of successful experience in business management, customer service and human relations with positive thinking and training.

Liza is currently a manager at a surplus store under the Lighthouse Mission, in Clovis, NM. She finds honesty, creativity and dedication to be the most valuable qualities for success for running a business and personal life.

Liza loves to be around family. She is a mother of 1 daughter, 2 sons, and grandmother of 14 grandchildren. She is blessed and highly favored to share the experience of love.

She enjoys helping people in many facets of life. She loves being by the water, arts and crafts, reading, and traveling. Her goals are to share the Gospel to the fullest in this world we live in today. 1 Thessalonians 5:111

Ruth

As I pondered on the Book of Ruth and seen the parallel between Ruth and I, was so vivid as how God has loved us to be the women of Proverbs 31. The beauty of love, meekness and devotedness to the experiences of our lives, to put people before us and carry it to the end, was sustainable to our goals. The relationships that grew from our desires to show that God is real in all our lives enter twine us with Christ Jesus and showed us that it's the inheritance of the Almighty. Having that knowledge as we know we are adopted into the kingdom and know the distinction of our walk in His will.

In Ruth the first chapter it speaks about a famine, a famine that was sent by the Lord upon Israel as a judgement because of spiritual declension. Into the country of Moab, Elimelech and Naomi and their sons Mahlon and Chilion. They came into the land of Moab and Elimelech died, and Naomi was left with her two sons, and they married Orpah and Ruth, then they dealt there ten years.

To be out of the Will of God always brings suffering. So, it was forbidden in the Law for a Hebrew to marry a Moabite woman, but a Moabite, because of being cursed by God, was forbidden to enter the congregation of the Lord. In this we see that we as humans make decisions and have to deal with the consequences of our lives, so we have to ask ourselves before we endure the decisions in our lives? What is the right thing to do? In the suffering it's very easy, spiritually speaking to go into wrong directions; however, very hard to leave that wrong direction in order to come back to the right way.

Then Naomi arose and return to the country of Moab, where she took her daughters in laws, Ruth and Orpah; with her and told them to go back home with their families, to their mother's home. Where she stated the Lord deal kindly with you as you have dealt with the dead and with me.

It seems that Naomi, at least at this stage, had so little faith in the promises of God and such a poor experience as a result of her own disobedience that she discouraged her daughter in laws from returning with her, then she should not have done, however, the same faithless that caused her and her family to leave Israel's plague her still. But as we shall see when she does return to Israel, her faith will begin to come back. Moab was not the place of faith, as the world system is never the place of faith. Israel was the place of faith, and so it presently, spiritually speaking. And this is where I see the faith that Ruth had, that she's stood by, even though Orpah left to go back home, but Ruth stood in a unshakable faith and stood by her mother-in-law. This is when we ask ourselves, do we walk by faith and not by sight?

Where Orpah leaves back to her people, we never hear from her again. V 15: And she (Naomi) said, Behold, your sister-in-law is gone back unto her people, and unto her gods: return thou after your sister-in-law. From that statement and to her gods, it is obvious that the great contending factor here was the gods of Moab versus the God of Israel, Orpah chose "her gods" and miss the greatest thing that could ever happen to any individual- Eternal Life.

In essence, Naomi asked Ruth, if that is what she's going to do as well, exactly as to what Naomi had in mind, we can only guess it seems that she didn't want to promise them things that she could not fulfill. This seems to have been her intention, but yet at all her faith, it seems with very, very low. V16: and Ruth said, Intreat me not to leave you or to return from following after you, for where you go, I will go, and where you Lodge, I will Lodge; your people shall be my people, and your God, my God, V 17: Where you die, will I die, and there will I be buried: the Lord do so to me, and more also, if ought, but death part you and me. This has to be one of the greatest statements, one of the greatest affirmations of salvation found in the entirety of the word of God.

In essence, it is that which must characterize all who come to Christ. In this consecration, there is no looking back, the die is cast, she will forever turn her back on the world of idolatry and rebellion against God, she will forever throw in her lot with those who worship the Lord of glory. Even when she dies, she does not want to be sent back to Moab, but rather buried in the Land of Israel, where she was.

She cut all ties with the past, even her family and everything else period, this is exactly the consecration that is demanded by God of all who come to him period, anything less constitutes no salvation at all. This is the steadfast mind that must be the character of every Believer. But Naomi's call as she sees herself, poorly dealt with in the Lord, she did not see the blessing that she had at all. So, where she seen empty: it was faith that seen it full.

Then they went to Bethlehem in the beginning of barley harvest. This was April, Passover time. In effect, the Holy Spirit is saying, "When I see the Blood, I will Passover you" There is no sin the Blood cannot cover. There is no life the cleansing of the Blood cannot change. It will change Ruth; it can change us.

In Chapter 2 states that Naomi had a Kinsman of her husband's, a mighty man of wealth, of the family of Elimelech; and his name was Boaz. There is one Hebrew word for "Kinsman" and "Redeemer", for he only had "the right to redeem" who was a Kinsman. Hence, it was necessary that the Lord Jesus Christ should become Man in order to redeem man. V2: and Ruth, the Moabitess said unto Noemi, "Let me now go to the field and glean ears of corn after him in whose sight I shall find grace." And she said unto her, "Go, my daughter." This portrays the fact that Ruth was poverty stricken. The welfare system of Israel in that day, which was given by God in the law of Moses, stated that the poor, during the harvest, could go into the fields and glean the leavings. In this Law, the reapers were instructed to not glean the corners of the field, and to leave a little something along the way.

We find that Ruth, although a beautiful young lady was not averse to hard work; those who are, are seldom if ever used by the Lord. Of course, the Holy Spirit was guiding her all the way. She did not know Boaz, but the Lord did. When the Lord plans for us, beautiful things result; when we plan for ourselves, there are no positive results period.

The favor of God is so splendid, and his grace and mercy are wonderful. As we see the favor Boaz had for Ruth was gentle and true. Boaz was very wealthy man. He was the Tribe of Judah, and in the direct line of the Messiah. And Ruth would be the great-grandmother of David, and, thereby, of the Son of David. The beauty of Ruth and her faith...to Pray. And Boaz, after being made aware of Ruth, and being introduced to her, now shoes her favor. Boaz had done far more than merely take notice of her. Her actions toward him denotes humility, a trait, incidentally, enjoyed by precious few. Boaz has already made it clear that he had already been informed of her consecration as a proselyte to the Hebrew faith, and her decision to leave her own people, her natives land and gods. He then pronounced a blessing from God upon her. In his own way, Boaz welcomes Ruth into the Family of God. But Ruth doesn't actually know who Boaz is. In the Kinsman position was one before Boaz and it was by law if that one refused, the next Kinsman had the position.

The instructions are very vital to us all. In Ruth, obeying Naomi to get ready and lay at Boaz feet. As she done, in this type of instance, Naomi has a type of the Holy Spirit, who seeks our good. His business is to ever lead us to Christ. In other words, don't relate to anyone what happened last night. There was no impropriety in Ruth's action. It was the Law and custom of the time. To draw a portion of the kinsman's mantle over one was the legal way of claiming protection and Redemption. Ruth affected this with great delicacy and skill. She chose a public place, such as a threshing floor, where many persons were present: but not to embarrass Boaz, but to give him liberty to act as he wished, she made her claim under the cover of darkness. Boaz, whose character commands admiration, immediately responds to her faith and love. How beautiful is a relationship that's positive and true. With my experiences I had to truly wait on the Lord for His answer. Amen.

The inheritance was so great. Thus Ruth, a "wild olive tree", was grafted into, and became a partaker of, "the root and fatness of the olive tree". But she could not boast that this was due to any commanding personal claim; all she could say was, "Why have I found grace in your eyes, seeing I am a Gentile?" Then they would marry, and the Prophecy continued. Bethlehem will forever be famous; the reason is that the son of David, the great descendant of Ruth, would be born in Bethlehem, some 1,200 years later. How beautifully and wondrously this Prophecy has come to pass.

Naomi raises the baby, Obed. And Ruth's little son, who is the kinsman referred to, the nearest kinsmen, still nearer than Boaz. To be sure, the child, who was the ancestor of David, and, ultimately, the Son of David, is linked to fame in a greater way than ever than these women could think. And the geology continuous until Jesus Christ.

We are so blessed and highly favored. And to see all this coming to prophesy and us as women to know that we are in His grace and mercy, can carry on as we listen to the Holy Spirit and know that we are the bloodline of the Most High.

To see myself in Ruth is an honor as I was raised by grandparents and learned to maintain morels and scruples and all done in knowing God, was so beautiful. Even as a young mother striving to survive and see trials and tribulations, was just knowing that they God all things are possible, amen! Ask yourselves where you stand in life and relationships and question your spiritual road. I pray for each and every one of you... In Jesus Christ name. 🙏

Reflection and Answer

So, ask oneself; where is the significance of the work of the Holy Spirit to change your empty to full?

_____
_____
_____
_____
_____

What is the virtuous favor?

_____
_____
_____
_____

Ask yourself; where do I stand in God's will in today's day?

_____
_____
_____

BLUEPRINTS FROM HEAVEN-WOMEN IN THE BIBLE EDITION BOOK 2| 2022
DEVOTION & COLABORATION

_____

_____

Where do I lay with my significant other?

_____

_____

_____

_____

_____

Coach Sheila Powell

Candace of Meroe

Candace of Meroe was known as the Queen of the "Ethiopians" or best known as the 'Queen Mother.' Candace, also referred to herself as the "Son of Ra'. Her kingdom expanded from Africa to the south of Asia. She was a fierce leader in battle and under her guidance her kingdom flourished and expanded. Her most famous battles were holding back the Roman Empire from invading her kingdom of Kusch. She fought off Alexander the Great which led the Roman forces to retreat. Candace even went as far as cutting off the statue head of Augusta and burned it under her temple. In return she gained the respect of her followers.

In the book of Acts 8:27-36, Candace is mentioned as sending her most trusted treasured advisor 'Eunuch.' Which in reference is a castrated man that protects the king's wives and concubines. The Eunuch came to Jerusalem to worship, when he met the Apostle Philip. Philip helped translate a scroll written by the prophet Esaias. As They traveled, the Apostle continued to read scripture and preach to the Eunuch about the teachings of Jesus. During the short travel they approached certain water and the Eunuch asked for Philip to baptize him. The Eunuch commanded the chariot to stop, and they went to the water, and Philip baptized him. Immediately after the baptism, the Spirit of the Lord whisk the Apostle Philip up into the sky and the Eunuch rejoiced.

Once the eunuch returned to Kusch, the Queen converted to Christianity. Therefore, the whole region that she ruled converted from worshiping Egyptian gods to Christianity.

Family and Respect

I believe that everyone should be treated fairly and with respect, no matter who they are. I believe material things that are owned by people should be treated the same way. Just like Candace, I'm very protected by my family and I believe in protecting my marriage, children and grandchildren. My aunts, uncles, cousins, nieces and nephews are also my family and I love them all the same and will do all that I can for them. Example: I have assisted in raising my first cousin's children while she was going through medical issues caused by Lupus. Her two sons lived with I, my husband, and our three children for several years. When her oldest son became a senior in high school, she became well enough to take care of them again. She eventually had a daughter. This was a true blessing,

Being married, raising five children, while working an eight-hour job, attending sporting events, cheerleading camps, vacations and going to college full time. And then, graduating from college with an associates and bachelor's degree was extremely hard but rewarding. With raising the kids, teaching them how to take care of themselves, their items, and the house. You want them to take pride in themselves, keep them uplifted and encouraged. When they walk out the door, they are a reflection of you, and you want people to know that God has them covered and they are walking among kings and queens. Although, during the years it was challenging, with prayer and the will, determination and strength it was rewarding.

As for the reminder of the family, I continue to love and help them as needed and they are with me. We have family dinners, and I go to doctor's appointments with parents, aunts, grandchildren and cousins. I often find myself not taking care of myself because I want to take care of everyone else. Candace lost an eye during one of her fierce battles. Even when she lost the eye; she continued to govern her kingdom and made sure it flourished.

I have Lupus, Wernicke encephalopathy, stage 2 kidney failure and Addison's disease. In April of 2010, I lost my youngest son Dominique in a car accident. He was a senior in high school and a star athlete, but I continue to love and advocate for my family, friends and others that may need my help. I'm truly blessed to be able to use the gifts that were given to me by God and the fight to continue no matter how I may be feeling.

I myself went back to college making sure that I would be able to work jobs that would bring in income to help sustain my family and allow me to work only one job, instead of two. It's very important to me to enjoy my family. I'm truly grateful for all that I have despite the stumbling blocks.

Trust

Knowing who you can and cannot trust is a difficult task. It takes a lot of trial and error before you can actually learn who holds your true allegiance to your agenda. Candace sent a spy into Alexander the Great camp before having an official meeting with him. This spy painted a portrait of Alexander and brought it back to Candace. She studied the portrait and when he snuck into her home; she met him and surprised him by calling him by his name. This began a love affair between the two great leaders.

Like Candace, I always like to know a little something about people before I meet with them. I sit back and let people talk without interrupting. You can learn a lot by just listening to people talk about themselves and others. I teach my grandchildren that you don't always have to be the first one to speak unless it will give you an advantage, silence can also be your friend.

I take time to learn and enjoy what is most important for everyone and make sure needs are met and that everyone is safe. She made sure that business and agriculture flourish in the region. Candace appeared to have one trusted friend or "Eunuch" that was mentioned in the Book of Acts. This is how her story was mentioned.

A question, how many friends do you really need? I have friends that appear to know everyone in the world, and I have friends that do not want more than maybe five true friends. Each friend has their own reasons for wanting more or less. As for me, I have less because of past experiences of having several friends and being betrayed for different reasons and it was just not worth the effort. Once I find that person, then it's a forever friendship, sisterhood or brotherhood. (Colossians 3:12).

Prayer

Father, God, I thank you for your grace and mercy that you've shown me throughout my years and still continue to live and breathe. You have been patient and kind, when I have not been obedient and respectful; you continue to show me love. As I laid in the hospital bed, thinking I was going to die, the only thing I knew how to do was call out your name and when I did, I woke up and the doctors said, "you're going to be alright." Hallelujah, Hallelujah, glory to God!!! My life changed and I now know, you and only you could give me every and anything that I needed, but on your time.

I give you continuous praises every day and will not stop, until you decide to take me home. Even when the police came to tell me that my son Dominique was killed in a car accident, I gave you praises, thanking you for the 18 years that you gave to my family to love him. As I continue to love and honor you Jesus for giving your life for me so I can one day be able to spend eternity in glory; I obey and follow the commandments and teach what you and the Father has laid out for us to follow. In your precious name Jesus, amen and amen.

BLUEPRINTS FROM HEAVEN-WOMEN IN THE BIBLE EDITION BOOK 2| 2022
DEVOTION & COLABORATION

Prophetess Chavelia Carthen

Chavelia Cecilia Carthen was born in Albany, Georgia to Betty W. Smith and Shelly B. Smith. She is the oldest of 5 children. Chavelia is a member of New Direction Christian Church in Albany, Georgia. She currently resides in Clovis, New Mexico she was formerly employed for the State of New Mexico as a Career Consultant and K-Bee Homecare as its Human Resource Manager. She is currently owner of C & C Consulting, LLC in Clovis, New Mexico where she helps Individuals and Churches find funding resources as well as establishing 501(3) c status. Chavelia enjoys reading, writing, singing and meeting new people. Chavelia is in the process of opening a Soul Food Restaurant as well.

THE STORY OF GOMER

Women have been very important in the bible and played various roles from the beginning from Genesis to Revelations. These women have several backgrounds, are from many places and had various occupations. In the Book of HOSEA, God chooses a Jewish woman named Gomer daughter of Diablim to deliver a message and warn the Israelites, about their sins as Jews. The Israelites are committing all types of sins and are deep into Idolatry. They are committing fornication, adultery and worshipping idols and other gods.

In the book of HOSEA, God told a devout Christian believer, who is saved, loved the lord and lives for God. God allowed Hosea to marry Gomer a woman who was said, to be very sinful. She committed various sins, was talked about and criticized by her community in where she lived. It was said that Gomer was undoubtedly, a prostitute because she was sleeping with many men for money. Gomer was from the northern region of Israel. She is an immoral woman who was unfaithful to her husband in which God Hosea to marry.

This marriage was to represent the symbolism of Israel and God. The Lord had delivered the children of Israel into the promise land where that started them to committing various sins which were against his commandments given. In this marriage there were three children born to Hosea and Gomer. The children were Lo-Ammi, Lo-Ruhamah and Jezreel. These children were given names to represent the judgement of the people. Their first born was named Jezreel, which means "God Scatters" meaning that he would punish the house of Jehu.

Lo-Ammi was the last son, his name given by God meant "not my People". The Lord gave this name to show that he rejected the people of Israel because of their sins and said, "That these people are not mine and I am not their God." Whereas the second child was a girl named Lo-Ruhamah meaning "God having no mercy" because he withdrew his love from Israel. Gomer, Hosea's wife kept leaving him and committing adultery, but each time God told Hosea to go and bring her back. When she left, he had to pay fifteen shekels of Silver which is 0.38

pounds of Silver and a lethech of barley equivalent to a measure of barely. Although Hosea had to keep going after her because he was obedient to God, and he loved her. In him going back in spite of her committing adultery he still loved her. Just as God loved the people of Israel.

Hosea was a man to me like David, after God's own heart, he loved God so much that he obeyed him regardless as to how the people felt about his wife. God will always have a way for you to return unto him. The story of Gomer was simply a way to show that there are many Gomers in today's society. Yet, God's love is bigger, greater and stronger than anyone else's. It was stronger than Hosea's where God can bring us back to fulfill his purpose and love us. Gomer represented how unfaithful Israel was and how God uses Hosea(himself) to redeem her (Israel) because of his never-ending love. God uses the foolish things to confound the wise! Even using Gomer's sinful nature of her continuing to be unfaithful to Hosea. The lord proves his love continuously in everything he did for them and even to us now.

Although Gomer may have embarrassed Hosea and caused him to be heartbroken. Nevertheless, he continued to love her as God continues to love us without wavering. Hosea showed patience, compassion and never gave up on Gomer. As God shows us compassion, he showed his love for the people of

Israel. Hosea had a love for his wife that was unconditional because God gave him this type of love for Gomer. Hosea had a love for his wife which was unconditional because God gave him this kind of love-that he loved her without conditions only because he believed.

As with us as men and women we are we were bought with a price that Jesus died for our sins. "For God so loved the world that he gave his only begotten son" So, that we can have everlasting life. So, women if you are a Gomer remember God loves you unconditionally. My story is that I can relate to Gomer because I once was an adulteress, but my husband and God forgave me. Remember, that God loves you and will forgive you and throws it all into the sea of forgetfulness. Gomer represented God's People and the people had a covenant with God, where they were to have no other God's before them. As she was received by her husband with Love and forgiveness so are we forgiven by God.

Reflection and Answer

Why did God tell Hosea to marry Gomer?

_____

_____

_____

What does Gomer name mean in the Bible?

What was the significance of Gomer in this story?

BLUEPRINTS FROM HEAVEN-WOMEN IN THE BIBLE EDITION BOOK 2| 2022
DEVOTION & COLABORATION

Evangelist Rosalind Willis

Dr. Rosalind Willis (Coach Roz) The Birthing Purpose Coach is a stroke survivor and an 18-year Chron's survivor. She has a passion to serve and reach the lost at any cost. She has a passion to empower every person she encounters. Her quote is "As long as you got a pulse you got a purpose" She is an International Public Speaker, Domestic Violence Survivor and Advocate. She is a wife, mother of 6 and Nana of 13. She has been an Ordained Evangelist for 29 years and loves outreach ministry. She is a ministry educator, and CEO of several businesses. She is the Founder of BPMI Ladies Club Global Outreach a Non-profit Organization's that bring women from all walks of life together to help, support, uplift and give them life skills and tools to improve their lives.

Dr. Rosalind is a voice for the voiceless and she uses her own life as a testimony that no matter what comes your way you can survive. She hosts ladies' tea outreaches to bring women together for empowerment. She is affiliated with multiple female organizations.

Dr. Rosalind is An Educator, she teaches high school Student Success and Computer Lab (Plato). She is a member of International Society of Female professionals. She is a member of WWCA, she is the Lubbock State Chair for G100 Oneness & Wisdom Wing, she is A Global Ambassador for TGA, and she is The Global Executive Director for Celina Fashion Magazine. She is a

Global Ambassador for BPMI LADIES CLUB GLOBAL, she is a Global Diversity Leader for Face of Women of Hearts, and she is the US Representative for The New Country Birland.

Two Women Two Babies

"That's My Baby"

In this world that we live in you see so much about Mothers abandoning their children and leaving them for someone else to raise or take care of. I remember years ago hearing of a mother that drowned her children in a van. Now there are thousands of stories of mothers intentionally killing their children for different reasons even some saying they do not know why they did it. This story in the bible states these two women was both prostitutes that lived in the same house maybe even the same room.

Now I was a teen Mom that used to sleep hard and wild all over the bed. My biggest fear was that if my baby layed with me once I gave birth to him that I would roll over on him. Let me tell you when I gave birth to my first child Terrance, I remember the first night of him being home with me. I layed him right beside me because I also had a fear of SIDS, so I did not want him in a crib or basinet. It still amazes me how God created me with a sensitivity to him. I would be sleeping and the slightest of sound I would wake up. I would sleep in one spot and would not even come close to laying on him. God completely protected me and him from that. God placed in me what my grandmother would call Mother's whit or sensitivity to my child. Now back to the story can you imagine a mother sleeping on their child until no life is left in his body? Then for that mother to pick that lifeless body up and lay it in the bosom of another mother and take the baby that is alive and lay it in her arms like nothing ever happened? Whew! That gives me chills with the thought of that. This woman had no connection to the dead or living baby. She did not care about the child she killed and did not care about the living child when the King said he could cut the baby in half she was ok with that. The enemy uses whoever allows him to. Clearly, he used this woman. But God in his wisdom spike to the King and he saw through the lies of the fake Mom. Only a true Mother feels for her child note; the true Mother does not have to be the one that gave birth. Having a baby does not mean you are a mother just like standing in a garage does not make you a car! God chooses the parents and I am a witness that God can and will give you the parents he wants you to have.

One day two women came to King Solomon, and one of them said: "Your Majesty, this woman and I live in the same house. Not long ago my baby was born at home, and three days later her baby was born. Nobody else was there with us. One night while we were all asleep, she rolled over on her baby, and he died. [20] Then while I was still asleep, she got up and took my son out of my bed. She put him in her bed, then she put her dead baby next to me. In the morning when I got up to feed my son, I saw that he was dead. But when I looked at him in the light, I knew he wasn't my son." "No!" the other woman shouted. "He was your son. My baby is alive!" "The dead baby is yours," the first woman yelled. "Mine is alive!" They argued back and forth in front of Solomon, until finally he said, "Both of you say this live baby is yours. Someone bring me a sword." A sword was brought, and Solomon ordered, "Cut the baby in half! That way each of you can have part of him." "Please don't kill my son," the baby's mother screamed. "Your Majesty, I love him very much, but give him to her. Just don't kill him." The other woman shouted, "Go ahead and cut him in half. Then neither of us will have the baby." [7] Solomon said, "Don't kill the baby." Then he pointed to the first woman, "She is his real mother. Give the baby to her." Everyone in Israel was amazed when they heard how Solomon had made his decision.

They realized that God had given him wisdom to judge fairly. (1 Kings 3:16-28 NIV Holy Bible from: www.biblegateway.com)

The job of the enemy is to kill steal and destroy and he wants to steal your living dream and replace it with a dead one! Yes, you heard me clearly, that dream, vision, baby, and/or book that you have had kicking inside of you he wants to kill! But the devil is a liar! I cancel the assignment of the enemy off your life. I Decree and Declare that Every dream, vision, baby, business that you have living inside of you will live and not die, in Jesus Name. Do not give up on your dream, vision, business, ministry, and/or baby. It is your time and no devil in hell can stop you!

Prayer: Father God. In the Name of Jesus, I pray that every hand that touches this workbook/devotional is changed for the better. I pray that every dream, vision, business, book, ministry, and baby be born, healthy, and prosperous. I cancel every assignment of the enemy off of every person's life that will read this devotional. I speak deliverance, healing, restoration, and peace. In Jesus Name, I pray. Amen.

Reflection and Answer

1. HAVE YOU EVER HAD A DREAM OR DESIRE THAT SEEMED

BLUEPRINTS FROM HEAVEN-WOMEN IN THE BIBLE EDITION BOOK 2| 2022
DEVOTION & COLABORATION

IMPOSSIBLE?

_____
_____
_____
_____
_____

2. WHAT DID YOU DO?

_____
_____
_____
_____
_____

3. IN WHICH WAYS CAN YOU RELATE TO THIS STORY?

_____
_____
_____
_____
_____

4. WHAT HAVE YOU PRAYED FOR IN YOUR LIFE AND SEEN GOD ANSWER YOUR PRAYER?

_____

_____

_____

_____

_____

5. DO YOU BELIEVE THAT GOD CAN RESTORE EVERYTHING THE enemy STOLE FROM YOU? AND HOW?

_____

_____

_____

_____

-DECLARATIONS

_____

_____

_____

_____

_____

_____

Evangelist Rosalind Willis

Coach Roz: "The Birthing Purpose Coach"

www.trbirthingbookspublishing.site

trbithingbookspubishing@gmail.com

325 864 3714

For speaking engagements, conferences, revivals and workshops.

References

All scriptures in this devotional came from the Holy Bible, the Word of God: (King James Version, NIV Version, NLV Version)

www.biblegateway.com

Notes

Made in the USA
Coppell, TX
25 May 2024

32719301R00125